101 Ways to Get Into Heaven

 *A Practical Guide*

by

Blaze Lovejoy & Ben Peller

Photographs by Stephanie Shepherd

Copyright © 2009 Blaze Lovejoy & Ben Peller

Photographs by Stephanie Shepherd

Additional photos and illustrations, cover and book design by Blaze Lovejoy. Stray dog photo by Joey Laguafina. Peller author photo by William Judd, ray of light photo by Bonnie Carroll

ALGONQUIN ROUND TABLE PUBLISHING

This edition published by Algonquin Round Table Publishing, 2015

ISBN-13: -978-0692513583

All rights reserved.

10: 0692513582

ACKNOWLEDGMENTS

Blaze Lovejoy would like to thank Stephanie Shepherd and the family of Ben Peller for agreeing to this publication.

Net profits from the sale of this book will be donated to NAMI, the National Alliance on Mental Illness, in recognition of their valuable efforts to provide support, education and advocacy for those in need. They may be found online at www.nami.org.

·

This book is dedicated to the memory of Ben Peller, who got into Heaven far sooner than everyone would have liked.

CONTENTS

About this book

How to use this book

Tracking your progress

1... be a responsible snowflake

2... click and save

3... bake a pie for your neighbor

4... give blood, sweat, or tears

5... drink tea instead of dropping a nuclear bomb

6... be open to family that may not be blood related

7... commune with nature

8... contemplate the problems of the world

9... plant lots of trees

10... give people the benefit of the doubt

11... be brutally honest with someone

12... if you see someone crying, ask them what's wrong

13... don't let the past or future haunt your present

14... make mistakes

15... watch a movie and discuss it with your friends

16... change your opinion of someone

17... question war

18... treat those older than you as people, not "old people"

19... swallow your pride

20... find your pace

21... don't be afraid to be weird

22... tidy up

23...go to the peace table

24... write an unhappy person a note from a secret admirer

25... pray or meditate

26... don't die rich

27... grow wealth for positive purposes

28... forgive someone

29... dispel prejudice

30... look around at least once a day and say "thank you"

31... climb a mountain, literal or metaphorical

32... treat a stranger as you would your favorite animal

33... remember a loved one, and do something in their honor

34... feed your gratitude instead of your despair

35... eat less cows

36... enlarge your comfort zone

37... adopt a child

38... sponsor a third world child

39... be aware of what lies above and beneath

40... give an anonymous gift to someone you're angry at

41... nurse a sick person – even if they have cooties

42... believe in a dream

43... dream big

44a... help a stray animal to a no-kill rescue center

44b... rescue an animal

45... go carbon neutral

46... throw a joke instead of an insult

47... question your intolerance of others

48... stitch up someone's stuffed animal

49... document another's life

50... hug someone, even if it's yourself   78

51... don't ever become too powerful to look up to another   80

52... *ride a bicycle at least once a week   81*

53... *appreciate your smallness in the depth of infinity   82*

54... *consider your impact within the space of one lifetime   83*

55... *learn about a religion different than your own   84*

56... *tell a child you love them   85*

57... *kiss a polar bear   86*

58... *seek the highest good in any situation*

59... *let a person younger than yourself know that they're cool*

60... *learn sign language*

61... *if a work of art affects you profoundly, write the creator*

62... *vote for something*

63... *respect your fellow earthlings*

64... *believe in aliens*

65... *be really good at just one thing*

66... *take pride in what you do*

67... *retain your innocence*

68... *massage a blade of grass*

69... *live longer by devoting your life*

70... *give a piece of handmade art to someone*

71... *learn CPR*

72... *laugh easily*

73... give the gift of good will for the holidays

74... stress more or less

75... clean your granny's curtain rail of dust

76...feel free to sing, whistle, and dance (and not only in the shower)

77... elevate consciousness

78... host a fundraising party

79... teach a child something

80... lay your vulnerability on the table

81... vent at someone before you actually see them

82... study quantum physics

83... politely refuse a telemarketer, and then wish them a great night

84... accept help when you need it, offer help when you don't

85... take an eco-vacation

86... attune yourself to the elevation of planetary consciousness

87... eat good food, but don't forget to nourish your soul

88... whatever your gifts may be, think of ways to give back

89... let go

90... passionately declare your love for someone

91... create sacred space for your home and family

92... shop wisely

93... find your point of epiphany

94... feed a hungry person

95... share your thoughts in order that others may share theirs

96... go on a complaint-free diet

97... try to understand something you really hate about someone

98... write your leaders

99... ask God to help with the vacuuming

100... accept that you are one day going to pass on from this life

101... experience Heaven in the moment

About the authors

Spirit level chart

Angel tokens

Thank you

ABOUT THIS BOOK

Who doesn't want to get into Heaven? Fairly much all the big religions believe in it in some form or another. Everyone agrees that it's Paradise – and once they head over there, people rarely ever come back.

The 101 things you'll find in this book are action-oriented activities that you can do to have a direct and positive effect on the people and the world around you. The book is intended as a practical guide to get a fast-track ticket into Heaven.

If you're already on your way, this will be a great tool to consolidate the process. You'll find tips and suggestions that are fun to do and your whole global family will love! If you're not sure of your chances, don't worry. No matter how many bad things you've done, once you start implementing the strategies we suggest, you will feel the weight of your past lifting, and we can get you a passage into Heaven, no questions asked.

In fact, we are so confident that our recommendations will get you into Heaven, we guarantee it! If it doesn't work out for you, call us collect from the Other Place, and not only will we grant you a full refund on your purchase, we'll see if we can't put in a good word for you!

Also, don't feel left out if you don't believe in Heaven, or think you've a lot of life to live before you worry about getting there - this is no problem! You can simply work through this book in the knowledge that each action you take will enhance your life, and that of others.

HOW TO USE THIS BOOK

If you're reading this book, you may already be performing some of the obvious practices that people do on their spiritual path; going to worship, studying religious texts, etc. These things are indubitably good, but are extra-curricular to this book. There are plenty of other places you can get instruction in such matters. We won't even touch on them, not to be neglectful of their importance, but because we'll assume you've got a handle on them and are looking for fresh ideas. We also designed this so that regardless of what you believe, you will find some incredible things to do in here that will benefit others and nourish your soul.

This book is a workbook, but does not have to be used sequentially. Some suggestions will be easier for you than others. Do the ones that are most appropriate to you first. If you're an adventurous type, you may find you like to open the book at random. Alternately, if you really love a challenge, work through cover to cover. Try to do just one thing daily. This latter will really improve your odds of getting into Heaven exponentially!

Also important to using this book successfully are the *"Spirit Level"*™ chart and *"Angel Tokens."*™ that you'll find in the back.

TRACKING YOUR PROGRESS

As you work through this book, you can add the Angel Tokens to the Spirit Level chart to track your progress up the chart. We had hoped to provide you with a "peel and stick" sheet of tokens, but we're a bit low-tech, so go ahead and scribble your own on there! Keep your chart in a prominent place; on your fridge, say, or above your desk, as a visual reminder of how your karma is improving.

We suggest you don't start by smattering the chart with angels from your previous deeds, but start afresh, so that the chart checks your future progress, not your past.

Start at the bottom left corner of the chart, and work from row to row. At the end of each row is a suggested reward to yourself for a job well done. Hopefully just the joy of doing a good deed will be enough incentive, but we want you to congratulate yourself on your progress, also.

Each item listed in the book has an angel rating. Most of the entries have a low rating, because they are actions that can be repeated and are of benefit every time. If you complete a particularly meritorious action, you'll get a Fat Angel!

The fat ones are worth five of the little ones.

Some of the entries in the book are very

concrete suggestions, others are more contemplative. Both are fine, but as far as the latter, so's you don't feel we're selling you a list of anodyne platitudes, we've been careful to include *"Practical Action"* underneath, that you can complete and quickly earn your Angel Token.

With careful diligence, you should find your angels fluttering swiftly up the chart toward the Heavenly Realm. But what if you have good intentions, yet find it impossible to progress? Do not despair. Sometimes people are genuinely oppressed by their circumstances, and due to commitments of family, work, incarceration, etc., cannot actualize their gifts. Their level of realization may still be strong. Circumstances may oppress the workday and the wallet, but they do not have to oppress the spirit. If you hold a good intention in your heart for long enough, without it finding a means of expression, award yourself a Grace Token and stick it to one of the squares where the Angels go. (You're on an honors system with all this. Use some discernment as far as Grace. If you're halfway to Heaven on Grace Tokens, and you don't have a major disability, you may be procrastinating.)

Once your chart has progressed to the Heavenly Realm, know that your soul is in good shape. But you don't have to stop there. There are many levels to Heaven and it is beautiful to rise up!

You can "like" us on Facebook, as "101 Ways to Get Into Heaven." Do message us with your thoughts, comments and karmic accomplishments! We would love to hear from you! It would be great if you could help us create a virtual community for people like yourself, who are taking control of their ascent to Heaven.

When you attain the 7th level of Heaven, you are one of our heroes!! We definitely want to hear from you, and maybe you can even share your story to help inspire others!

Guilty conscience? Check the conscience meter at the bottom of the chart. Whenever you accomplish a good deed that you think could equivocate with one of your bad deeds, add an Absolution Sticker to one of the checked boxes. Participation in this section of the chart, however, is completely optional. Of course your progress is a subjective measurement; we don't know what was plaguing your conscience before you started with the program, and it is certainly not for mortals to judge! You may feel bad about it, but we'd like to think that if you have truly had a change of heart, this will get you a long way on the path to Heaven.

Of course, an approach as pragmatic as this is very tongue-in-cheek, but what we really want you to do is to go out there and have fun with it. Be aware that the beauty of any journey isn't necessarily the arrival; it's how much you can experience and how many lives you can affect on your way there. You are a bright, blessed soul, and as this book comes from our souls to yours, and we hope it offers you new ways to shine! Go forth and make the world a better place!

101 Ways to Get Into Heaven

1... *be a responsible snowflake*

As human beings, we have several things in common with snowflakes. There is not one other person in the world exactly like us. We have a limited lifetime before we pass on and our bodies go back to nature. Unlike snowflakes however, we have the capacity to guide our own course. Ultimately it is we who choose to rise or merely accept falling. It has been said that no individual snowflake in an avalanche ever feels responsibility. Well, snowflakes may not be able to feel responsibility, but we as human beings can. If you feel an injustice is being done, act to stop it. Speak up for those who may be being repressed. Celebrate a kind act. If a windfall comes your way, share and join with others. Above all, should you ever find yourself feeling swept along and helpless, be it by an irredeemable past, a seemingly impossible present, or an uncertain future, remember: you are a human being. You can be a responsible snowflake.

The Practical Action: Sit down for ten minutes and make a list of issues on which you are willing to "fall upward." Check out www.bigthink.com for intelligent discourse on hot topics.

- BP

Angel Rating: 1

2... *click and save*

How would you like to, every day, feed starving people and sheltered animals, protect rainforests, promote children's health and literacy, and fight breast cancer? All with a simple click of a button? Not only that, but this won't cost you a dime! Head to www.greatergood.com. There are hyperlinks to nine different causes. Visitors clicks are tabulated daily, and each one is a voice counted to help these causes. This site is kept in business through its sponsors, who pay for the donations. They also offer many goods and services, some esoteric and some quite practical. This is one of those tickets to Heaven that's almost too good to be true. It takes only thirty seconds out of a day and helps innumerable people. The Internet is a vast and wild creature, and like any uncharted territory there are dangers and viruses. But there are also beneficial and heartwarming "sites" to behold. This is one of them.

The Practical Action: *Each day you log on to a computer, make this site the first site you head to. Before your email, before the trashy celebrity news, before any other sites.*

- BP

Angel Rating: 1-FAT!

One for clicking for a week:

A fat one for a year:

3... bake a pie for your neighbor

What good is the global village without a local community? When we speak of neighbors, we don't have to be talking about actual next-door neighbors, but those who we share a block with. Or a town with. Or a country with... you get the idea. We are in effect all neighbors here on this planet. But we can start humbly by reaching out to those around us, and creating a sense of family and safety in a world that's become increasingly lonely and isolated. I must confess that I rarely bake pies because I'm no good with crusts. However I do support every bake sale, and I try and be nice to those around me.

Ayurvedic medicine is a system of holistic health care that goes back to ancient India. In this tradition, it is believed that by preparing food with good spirit, we bestow positive energy on all who eat it. Can you bake a lot of love into a pie? I'd like to think so!

The Practical Action: *Next time you find yourself baking a pie (or any kind of treat), feel free to bake a bit extra for your neighbor, regardless of whether this neighbor lives next door to you or hundreds of miles away.*

- BL

Angel Rating: 1

4... *give blood, sweat, or tears*

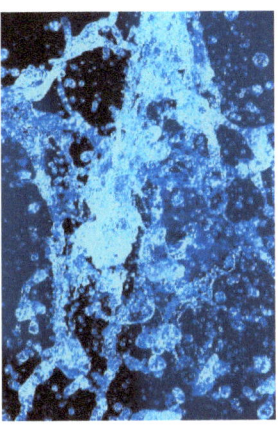

What better way to share your blessing of life with another than to give your own blood. Squeamish? I certainly was my first time. By the fifth time I'd gotten a bit better. After ten times it was and still is a snap. You've got blood. You can give it for free and save a life!

Or sweat. Participate in a walk for a good cause, such as finding a cure for breast cancer. This is especially good if you're a couch potato, as many of these charity walks are on Sunday and instead of eating chips and watching "the game," you can get exercise, help others, and build up karma points for the office sports pool.

And tears. Tears are also a natural secretion, and a highly beneficial one. Be they shed for a loved one, a work of art, or a random article in the paper, they are not only a great release but also can serve as a reminder to others how much you care about them.

The Practical Action: *The next time you hear of a blood drive, sign up. If you don't hear about one within a month, seek out your local Red Cross donation center. The same goes for a walk for a cause. As far as tears go, if whenever you shed them you do so honestly, that's enough.*

- BP

Angel Rating: 1

5... drink tea instead of dropping a nuclear bomb

I have to get the tea thing in 'cause I'm English, not to mention Chinese too, and we do love a spot of tea. In the book *"No Destination,"* Satish Kumar writes of two young men who in 1962 went on a "Pilgrimage for Peace" from India to the four corners of the nuclear world: Moscow, Paris, London, and Washington, D.C.. Vinoba Bhave, a contemporary of Gandhi's, gave them two gifts: to be penniless wherever they walked, and to be vegetarian. I hate to think what his Christmas list looked like.

Anyway, on their way to Moscow they met a woman outside a tea factory. She gave them four tea bags, to be given to each of the leaders of the four nuclear powers with the message: "When you think you need to press the button, stop for a minute and have a fresh cup of tea." With no money, reliant on the kindness of strangers, they walked far enough to deliver "peace tea" to all four leaders. Can tea prevent a nuclear holocaust? All I can say is, we've survived thus far. In England, there's a lot of tea consumed, and it holds the fabric of society together. The ritual has a commonality that bonds people, in cheeriness and chat. Whatever happens, be assured the British will keep brewing. It saw us through the Blitz. It's seen us through the Cold War, and it will no doubt help us cope with whatever challenges the future may bring.

The Practical Action: *Anytime you feel you're about to explode, stop and have a nice cup of tea. Works wonders.*

— BL

Angel Rating: 1

6... *be open to family that may not be blood related*

It's true that family is important, but sometimes those who unveil themselves as being most precious to us do not necessarily share our blood, genes, or skin color. There have been people in my life who have had a tremendously positive influence on me, and they're not necessarily biological family, but spiritual family. As I've been blessed with many people such as this in my life, I've also, on the flip side, had members of my supposed "blood family" who have been abusive and negative. Many of us have had dysfunctional childhoods, some much more so than others. Abusive behavior, be it physical, sexual, or verbal, is oftentimes handed down from one generation to the next. Don't be afraid to break the cycle. There has been much heartache and pain in the world because people have done what's "right for the family," such as keeping secrets bottled up and not being able to walk away from harmful situations. Be open to your spiritual family, people you may encounter in life who, though not connected by blood, are connected by something even stronger and more resilient: love.

- BP

The Practical Action: *If you love someone you're not blood related to and consider them a parent, a brother, a sister, or any other kind of relation, tell them so.*

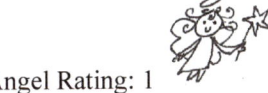

Angel Rating: 1

7... *commune with nature*

Anthropologist Gregory Bateson, who wrote "Steps to an Ecology of Mind" says, "The major problems in the world are the result of the difference between how Nature works and the way people think." It is good for our peace of mind to get out in Nature. Every living thing has an aura. Nature has so much to offer that we don't even consider. Outside of the city, we are surrounded by life, growth and positive vibrations. Did you know green is the most relaxing color to the eye? Kick back and listen to the grass growing, and the trees whispering.

You don't have to go a long way to commune with Nature. I have an arbor at the bottom of my garden that's shaded by a bamboo thicket. This is the place I repair to each morning for a bit of praying and meditating. Sitting there, I can see birds and butterflies, the occasional squirrel. The squirrels filch my avocados, (my second favorite food, next to chocolate) but I don't mind at all. One time I was blessed with a visit from a confused possum.

I still keep an altar in the house for bad weather, but I like it outside. Nobody knows I'm there, and it's so nice I feel like I'm getting away with something, somehow. Of course, it's completely paradoxical that I should feel that way - about one area of my life that's actually unspoiled!

The Practical Action: *Allot yourself some time in Nature, preferably alone, or else with a trusted friend. Allow yourself to quiet your mind, simply by listening to the Nature sounds. Work on distinguishing different sounds, the grass, the birds, the insects. Be aware that each of these is a living thing. Put your arms around a tree and feel the strength of its years. Go on, hug the tree!*

- BL

Angel Rating: 1-2

One for getting out in Nature. Two if you can really experience it!

8... *contemplate the problems of the world*

There was a big oversight made by both the science and religious communities back in the 60s when they first found out the Earth was warming. They failed to align themselves against a global sized problem. Of course, there's always been bad blood between the Darwis and the Creationists, but this is one of those areas where it would benefit everyone to acknowledge that science and religion can and do overlap. Nobel laureate Al Gore has said of the climate crisis, *"It is a moral and spiritual challenge to all of humanity. It is also our greatest opportunity to lift global consciousness to a higher level."*

Fortunately, there's also some indications of warming between the scientists and theologians. Many Southern Baptist leaders have signed on to "A Southern Baptist Declaration on the Environment and Climate Change." This document realizes that not all Christians accept the science behind global warming, but the threat is too grave to ignore.

Since Adam, we have been stewards of God's garden here on Earth. If we don't tend the garden right, things will die. Some people believe God would never let that happen. But remember that if God sent the flood once, He could certainly do it again. We've been messing up His planet, big time. There's no commandment against this, because Moses came before the Industrial Revolution, and really, humankind is grown enough that we ought to be able to figure it out for ourselves: Wrecking God's good Earth is a sin.

I don't mean to rant on about "sin" here, this is meant to be a positive book, but to any climate deniers out there, this is a very important point that we must all get our heads around.

101 Ways to Get Into Heaven

The Practical Action: *Read the news. Think. If you read the news on paper, recycle the paper. Recycle anything you can, be it from newspaper to cans to compost. Head to www.earthday.net and make every day Earth Day!*

- BL

Angel rating: 1-3:

   for contemplating

   for feeling affected on account of others

   for deciding to make a difference

9.... *plant lots of trees*

Trees are peaceable and help combat global warming. Everything about trees is a good thing. But we've lost more than half of the world's rainforest, along with the thousands of plant and animal species and tribes people who lived there. We can't possibly redress the balance, but every one of us should plant trees.

- If you want to get inspired to do your own tree planting, read *"The Man Who Planted Trees,"* by Jean Giono.

- To sponsor or volunteer for tree planting in North America, go to www.treepeople.org. You may want to give a tree for mothers' day, or a grove of trees to celebrate the birth of a child.

- Sponsoring trees in developing nations costs very little to do, and yields huge karmic rewards. Check out www.treesforthefuture.org. They can also sell you a moringa kit, so you can grow your own moringa tree. Moringa is a tree that yields protein-rich flowers and fruit, to sustainably feed starving people in the Third world. You can donate to reforest entire villages that have been devastated by the climate crisis. I did this for a gift to my son last Christmas, cost me just $480 for 5,000 trees, and we're so happy about it, I can't wait to do it again this year!

The Practical Action: *- Sponsor tree plantings or go out and plant trees. Do it in your backyard, in a schoolyard, or anywhere you see a space that a tree could call home.*

Angel Rating: 1-FAT

One for a single tree, 2 for a grove, a fat one for a forest.

10… give people the benefit of the doubt.

Just so's you know, my co-author, Ben, can get a little squirrelly sometimes. Yesterday we were stopped outside his apartment building, discussing relative merits of various ways to get into Heaven, when he got completely distracted by a beat-up yellow Volvo whizzing past. It had, apparently, whizzed past twice, and he was convinced the driver was casing the joint. (What he might have that's worth taking, I don't know, as Ben epitomizes the ideal of living simply, and to a pretty grungy extreme.) I'd just managed to get the conversation back on track, when there went the yellow Volvo again, driving completely erratically. Ben immediately concluded that the driver was a lunatic, and that the police should be called. I countered that maybe some poor, broke individual was out to see how the car drove. He brightened at this suggestion, remembering that there's a Volvo repair shop on the corner of his street.

Don't be like Ben, ha-ha! (Sorry, Ben!)

When you have a dubious thought about someone, stop it at the first thought, before it snowballs into something fearful! See if you can come up with an alternate explanation for their behavior. I'm not saying overlook the facts if someone's really out to rob you. But try and see the best in people. At the very least, this will make you more empathetic to why they're behaving badly. More than this, when you focus on people's good qualities, not only will your view of the world be more rosy, but you will interact with people in a more relaxed manner, and bring out the best in them.

The Practical Action: *Think of someone you're really not sure about. Make a list of their good and bad qualities (so far as you know them), and then a list of the things they're done that make you leery of them. List the reasons why these things turn you off. How much credence should you give to these things? Are some of them irrational or ego-driven? Make a list of plausible explanations for this person's behavior. You don't have to do anything with this list, it may just confirm a need to steer clear of this person! But see if your perception of them changes at all. You may find you can greet them more easily when you see them next!*

- BL

Angel Rating: 1

11... *be brutally honest with someone*

Selfish. Negative. Spoiled. Self-pitying. Egotistical. Madman. These are things, amongst others, I've been called over the years. More often than not, in my younger years, I shrugged them off to people who were either jealous or deluded. But as I grew older and someone would offer me a less than complimentary assessment, I tried to really look at it. People often corrected me on my language, as well. "Ben, it's just not classy to use the f-word every other sentence." This was told to me by someone I respected. I looked at my use of language and found that, well, I *did* use that word excessively. Other bad habits (see listed above) I've tried to counteract in my later years. As I've come to recognize that I, like most people, have faults of varying degrees, I've become very grateful to people who have pointed them out to me. That these folks are unguarded enough to be honest with me makes me feel even closer to them. No matter how it may sting at the time, to be brutally honest with someone is a demonstration that you care about them. I would like to point out that this Way should be reserved for more major issues. (i.e., Gentlemen, no matter how much you want to be honest with your wife/ladyfriend, we all know there's not a dress in this world that makes them look fat). -

BP

The Practical Action: *Use this way with responsibility, and when doing so be sure it is appropriately timed and invoked with a grace that will educate the recipient, not shame them. If there's no-one around that you can try this on right now, practice on yourself! Think of one thing that you'd really like to re-evaluate about yourself, and find one simple thing you can do to start to change it.*

Angel Rating: 1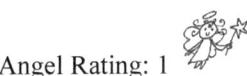

12... *if you see someone crying, ask what's wrong*

Who hasn't been down so low that sometimes reassurance, no matter who it may come from or how general its nature, makes a hearty difference for the simple reason it indicates someone is there for us and cares enough to bolster us (even if they may have to make a generous assumption of faith to do so).

I was on a bus once and there was an older woman crying softly to herself. People were uncomfortable and tried to avert their eyes as subtly as possible. I was one of those people. For ten uncomfortable minutes we all listened to this woman sobbing softly. She wasn't making a big production out of it. She was just in pain. I don't know what my fellow passengers were thinking, but I was strenuously telling myself that if I approached her I would just be interfering in her life, that I would be sticking my nose in someone else's business, that it wasn't my problem. I busied myself looking out the window but couldn't stop my eyes from wandering to her. Then she got up and exited the bus, eyes down, looking ashamed. I have no idea what happened to her, but there are times, more than I care to admit, when I think of her and wonder. Maybe writing this down will help not only you but me, the next time we see someone in pain, to be able to conquer the awkwardness of helping a stranger and acknowledging such blatant vulnerability.

The Practical Action: *The next person you see who's upset, ask them what's wrong. If you can do something about it, do. If not, listen to them. Sometimes that's enough.*

- BP

Angel Rating: 1

13... *don't let the past or future haunt your present*

When we worry over future uncertainties or regret our imperfect past, we lose the perfection of the present moment. The miracle of breathing, of being alive *at this moment.* Certainly it's not always easy to retain your present, but if one practices it enough, giving thanks for each breath, it becomes a natural act, as natural as breathing. Dr. Spencer Johnson wrote a book entitled *"The Precious Present."* It's definitely worth reading, about a discovery of a gift that is truly a gift that keeps on giving, as long as we are alive. Though we may be the victims of heartache or injustice, as long as we are alive we have the power to learn and grow from our current situation. But above all, what we have is precious. To live in the present moment is to never be bored. As Camus wrote in *"The Stranger,"* the person who truly lives one day of their lives and experiences every detail, will never be bored. Thornton Wilder in *"Our Town"* questioned if anyone ever truly appreciated their life, every minute of it, and opined: *"The poets do... some."* May everyone reading this embrace and live in their own unique present, and become poets.

The Practical Action: *Be in this moment as you read this, and smile at the wonder of that. You're not done yet. After one week, recount at least fifteen moments that you actually experienced fully. If you in fact did, you should be able to recall them. If not, keep practicing relishing every moment, the apparently good and the apparently bad.*

- BP

Angel Rating: 1

14... *make mistakes*

Mistakes and triumphs have one key characteristic in common: they are both preceded by action. I've spent many many hours discussing things with friends, co-workers, and random strangers. An oft repeated phrase is: "I've got this great idea for..." It's been said that "Man can not live by (insert preference) alone." Well, human beings certainly can't live on ideas alone. The first *Homo sapien* who had the idea of rubbing two stones together would never have discovered fire if they hadn't *acted* upon this inspiration. Ideas are vital, but the most life-changing idea in the world is worthless without action. Yes, you may make horrible mistakes, you may go through sufferings as you experience setback after setback. But as Joyce said, *"mistakes are the portals to discovery."* Too many people consider themselves a failure by giving up when in fact they have the power to remain in the game. As long as you're taking action, you can look anyone in the eye as an equal.

The Practical Action: *Embrace a past mistake as though it were a success. Consider what you wouldn't have learned had you not*

made that mistake. Wisdom sometimes comes with a price, something that Winston Churchill knew when he said success could be defined as "moving enthusiastically from one failure to the next."

- BP

Angel Rating: 1

15... *watch a movie and discuss it with your friends*

This is way too easy. We do this all the time just for fun.

Did you see the Wim Wenders film, *"Wings of Desire"*? A very lyrical story in which angels are hovering over Berlin, silently soothing the troubled hearts of its inhabitants. Also documenting in their little notebooks every time they witness mortals doing something that is close to God. Entries like: *"A passer-by, in the rain, folded her umbrella and was drenched."* It's my all-time favorite movie. I mention it here for the notebook angle; whenever we witness the spiritual in humanity, it's worth pausing to take note.

So when you're picking out that movie, don't think you can get away with renting *"Saw IV"* and merit a passage to Heaven. In fact, I actively encourage you not to pollute your psyche with that kind of crap. Find something uplifting, transcendent. Screenwriters, filmmakers, musicians, et al, may all direct their artistic expression toward a pure distillation of the human spirit. Seek this out, savor the feeling, and share it with your friends. This is a feeling we would all like to inhabit, all of the time.

If this is too artsy for you, get a copy of *"An Inconvenient Truth"* instead. Or anything of Michael Moore's. Or pass them out as Christmas or Hanukkah gifts. They're awesome.

- BL

Angel Rating: 1

16... *change your opinion of someone*

Preferably for the better, unless your opinion of them is considerably over inflated. Get out of that rut of believing that this or that aspect of a person is completely useless. When confronted with a grumpy, miserable person, try to visualize them as pleasant and joyous, and interact with them accordingly. You may just change their energy for the better, and if that fails, at least you'll feel better cause you're holding for them. And you might benefit the next person you meet!

The Practical Action: *Be on the lookout for the next person to piss you off. It may be a stranger, it may be a family member! Observe yourself if you mentally berate them or heap unpleasant labels on them. Hopefully you will catch yourself before you do so out loud! Then revise your paradigm. Be aware that inside that person, whether or not it is apparent, there are many seeds of kindness, love and wisdom. Treat them as if they had something important to impart to you.*

- BL

Angel Rating: 1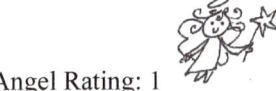

17... *question war*

It's an unpleasant fact that war has been not only with humans, but with all of nature for a very long time, and will likely continue to be. Is it possible to stop war on a global scale? Perhaps. But there have been wars such as World War II that have prevented madmen from slaughtering millions of more innocent lives. Wars have been fought for freedom, and wars have been fought for profit. War is indeed a terrible thing, but sometimes necessary. Because of war's steep costs on humanity and the world, it should always be questioned. True leaders should have not only the courage of their convictions but also the intelligence to support the reasons for their actions. Blind faith in a leader can be dangerous, particularly at a time when war is being proposed or engaged in. People who oppose wars aren't bad, people who support wars aren't bad; it is those who do either without question who are equally guilty of thoughtless behavior.

- BP

The Practical Action: *If there is a war occurring that you don't agree with, make your opposition known. However, learn from history and do not blame those who may be drafted or required to serve for a war they themselves may not even agree with.*

BL note: Actually, I'm dogmatic in my belief that war is always a bad thing. If you're a pacifist too, I think you're exempt from having to question war, as you've already given it some thought.

BP note: Just the fact that this Way is in the book is a case of Blaze and I agreeing to disagree, thus proving that harmony is always preferable to war.

Angel Rating: 2

18... *treat those older than you as people, not "old people"*

It's amazing how much older people can be much more aware of things than they let on. So the next time an elderly person acts "out of it" or "forgetful," just remember: they may be just pretending. My grandfather once told me it was a good idea to listen to people who'd been around longer than I, even if I didn't necessarily agree with them. Heaven knows I certainly didn't always agree with him, but I did listen to him, and I learned much. It doesn't matter if you're listening to a teacher, an older sibling, or a cantankerous grandfather (Kidding, Harold!) If anything, keep in mind that people older than we have often experienced situations we may have yet to encounter. Even if we disagree with their opinions and beliefs, we can learn from their mistakes. In my life I have known many wonderful people who are older than me who have taught me great lessons. On the other side of the coin, there have been those who have grown bitter shells and their cynic negativity stood as a warning indicator of the type of creature I never want to become. I'm grateful to both.

The Practical Action: Listen to the next person who tries to tell you something, particularly if they've got some years behind them. Learn from them, for better or worse.

- BP

Angel Rating: 1

19... *swallow your pride*

Pride is a natural secretion. Like a healthy sweat, it can make us feel good and also attract others, but if we put forth too much, the results are usually a bit off-putting. So feel free to, instead of allowing it to pour out of your mouth in the form of bragging, denial of mistakes, and blatant self-promoting, swallow it. There's a tale about an apprentice poet who finally was able to meet the writer who made him want to be a poet. The younger poet, who had already had some success with publication very early, was bursting with news about his accomplishments as the older writer poured them tea. As the older writer sipped his tea, he listened to the younger poet rattle off his achievements and how he was going to make a mark in the world of poetry. The older writer sipped his tea and refilled both his own glass and the glass of the younger poet's across the table. After the third time he did this, the younger poet's cup was overflowing so much it was beginning to drip down the table onto his lap. *"Excuse me,"* said the younger poet. *"My cup's overflowing."* The older poet calmly replied that it would then be wise to swallow some tea. The younger poet got it. His idol had been telling him, in a subtle way, to shut up and take a breath. Often, a pride-drenched rant will not impress, but repulse others. After all, there's no deodorant for excessive pride.

***The Practical Action:** The next time you find yourself boasting about an accomplishment to someone, pause. Ask the person about something they're the most proud of. Listen to their response and make it a mutual celebration.*

- BP

Angel Rating: 1

20... *find your pace*

A note on speed here: A lot of these New Agey books will tell you to slow down. If you're in a constant state of overwhelm, yes, you need to slow down. Or you may need to pare your load down, to do less things, more effectively.

But think about whether slowing down is the best thing for you. The pace of modern life is fast.* Personally I want to live to the fullest and do my best not to get left behind! The trick for me is to remain centered whilst doing and aim to go as full-tilt as I can without stressing.

At times when you're confident that you're on a good mission, this will help reduce the stress. It's amazing what we can achieve when the motivation is directed towards others and not ourselves. This is not a good time to sit around and do nothing, it's time to get out there and change the world for the better! Go forth. Don't forget to breathe. Slowly. Deeply. Keep the stillness in your Soul and the bustle in your butt.

*This may not apply to you at all if you're in a nice sleepy little village.

The Practical Action: *Give some thought to your speed of life. If you're overwhelmed, look at acquiring some time management skills. Each morning, write down an achievable, prioritized list of what you would like to accomplish during the day. Stick to the list and check each item off as it gets done.*

- BL

Angel Rating:1

21... *don't be afraid to be weird*

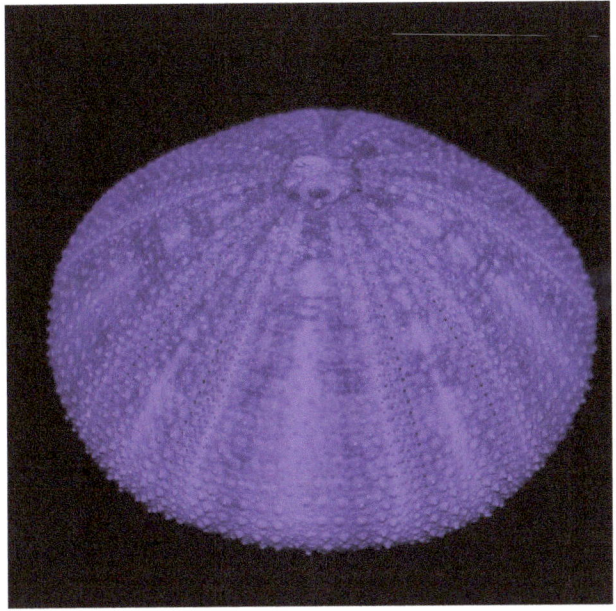

As human beings, imagination is one of our most powerful gifts. Never be afraid to be considered weird or out of the ordinary by imagining what may sound like sheer lunacy to others. Talk to yourself, exchange ideas with imaginary friends, attempt to invent whatever you may want. W hat may be folly to one person may be something another person spends their whole life trying to make happen. A person such as Gugielmo Marconi, who was the first inventor to actually transmit sounds through electromagnetic energy, thus making the telegraph possible and fueling further revelations such as radio, television, and the Internet. Or Nicolaus Copernicus, who endured rejection from the Catholic Church when he dared make the suggestion that earth's center was *not* the center of the universe. An original thinker who dared go against the beliefs of the time and comprehend that stars in the sky were in fact planets, that weather could be predicted, that the earth is round.

A famous author, when asked how he came up with ideas for his books, simply replied, *"I don't come up with them. They do."* When questioned who "they" were, the author just smiled. Being weird doesn't necessarily makes someone creative, but it certainly makes them interesting.

Speaking of weird authors, my co-author bought her son Xai a book entitled *"My Cat's Weird."* She explained to me that she purchased this book so that Xai would be unfazed by *her* weirdness. As her longtime friend, I can certainly sympathize with the lad. At the same time, he's a lucky child to have such a unique loving parent.

The Practical Action: *Should someone or some group call you weird or abnormal or anything that may bring about designs of the extraordinary, be sure to thank them. Then compliment them on being so utterly normal.*

- BP

Angel Rating: 1

22... *tidy up*

I'm not going to throw a *"Cleanliness is next to Godliness"* thing at you, but when you don't know what next to do, it might help to tidy up.

This probably doesn't seem like a way to get into Heaven, in fact it's more like a necessity. But an ordered environment facilitates clearer thoughts, better focus and more peace, happiness and success. Totally basic, but it's good feng shui!

As a writer, running a business and parenting a child, I frequently get into a buildup of paperwork where it's suddenly hard to function. It's wretched and overwhelming. After it's filed, I feel much better.

Don't overlook tidying up. Sometimes it's your mind that you must clear the clutter from. If you haven't mentally cleaned house in a while, be aware that this may be keeping you stuck in the past, entrenched in old ways of thinking and operating. Let it go. It's time to purge a bunch of stuff and open yourself to new influences.

The Practical Action: *Spring clean each New Year. If you lack time to clean house, just set aside an hour, and work on one room at a time. Also, try cleaning when you're talking on the phone.*

- BL

Angel Rating: 1

23... *go to the peace table*

When my son Xai was in preschool, if the children got into it with each other, they were sent to the Peace Table. The Peace Table was not a punishment, more an opportunity for them to work things out. Really, it was a plain old wooden table, with kid art and a peace sign painted on it, but symbolically it was a place where they had space to breathe through their anger, to talk through their feelings and to resolve their differences.

This was a whole lot better than when I was his age and would likely get slapped for misbehaving. I was very impressed at the confidence levels the children developed, and how good they were at sharing and socializing.

In our kitchen at home, we still keep a Peace Table, where we can go any time there's a dispute in the family. It's not just for Xai; if my husband loses his temper, he gets to sit there too! Lately, I've been thinking maybe I should try going there more often. I rarely lose my temper, but it might be a good way to air out those things that upset me and I really should discuss.

Actually, there's a bunch of stuff Xai gets taught in school that's way more important than what I was learning at his age. Cooperation, teamwork, counting to ten and unclenching your fists... He brings it home as artwork and activities, and I look at it not just as something to encourage him in, but something for us to learn from.

Of course, I wish all world leaders could go to the Peace Table and not leave until they've worked it out. I'm not in control of that, but I will say this: As adults, we must practice tolerance, patience, compassion. The more we create this as our center, the more we can empower our children to have good conflict resolution skills. As they get older, this will come in handy. It may even make the world more peaceful. The more we can get along, the happier everyone will be. It's so simple, a child can understand it.

The Practical Action: *Should you find yourself in the midst of an argument with someone, agree to retire to a nearby table, be it at home, in the employee's lounge, or a random park bench. Taking a moment to sit with someone serves as a reminder that they are a person, just like you, and helps foster reasonable resolutions instead of escalating accusations.*

- BL

Angel Rating: 1

This is a recurring angel! You get one just for setting a Peace Table up, and also one for every time you go to either this designated peace table or an improvisational one. (If you have a lot of issues, this could be a quick way to amass a lot of merit!)

24... *write an unhappy person a note from a secret admirer*

This is a totally quirky, odd one, but may help pass the time while you're stuck on an airplane, whatever. Say there's a self-neglected individual across the aisle from you, who's looking like her esteem's hit an all-time low. Write her a quick note. It doesn't have to be flowery or poetical, although if you have skills that way it's always a plus. Be sure to look for the admirable qualities that you see in her, look carefully (sidelong), they are surely there even if she can't see them. By mentioning specifics, your missive will come across as sincere, and not some kind of sick, cruel joke. Slip it on her seat while she's in the bathroom. Try and look all innocent while you observe to see if her mood brightens after.

I like this one because it's a random act of kindness that you don't take credit for; the stealth factor makes it seem kind of naughty. Also good for co-workers if you want to spread office cheer whilst keeping it to yourself. Keeping it to yourself is good for the ego, or should I say a good test for the ego. See how many good deeds you can get away with unnoticed. You'll presumably get your reward in Heaven, but this should not be your motivation; just try and do something nice.

The Practical Action: *This idea's just a jumping off point. See how many variations you can come up with, such as sending flowers to a co-worker going through a hard time, or mailing a good old fashioned Greeting Card (not an email) with handwritten best wishes to someone who's down...*

- BL

Angel Rating: 1

25... *pray or meditate*

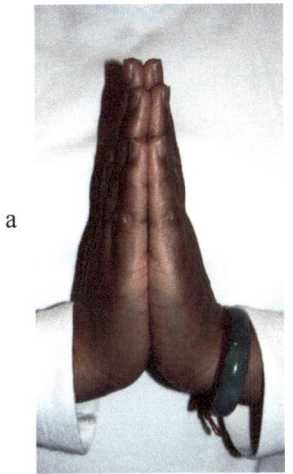

Chances are if you're reading this book you've already set aside your allotted time and are going at it on a daily basis. You already value your spiritual practice, and know it's a calming and centering piece of your routine - but there's one thing I'd like to emphasize here. Spiritual practice is called practice because it's just that – you're practicing in order to integrate spirituality into every area of your life.

When you pray and meditate, you may experience moments of clarity, compassion, illumination. You can't, of course, hold onto such moments; they belong to the Divine. But by opening yourself through prayer and meditation, you may become more a vessel for the Divine. When you are focused in that way, you create a sacred space in and around yourself. Your task, when you go out into the world, is to take it out into the world with you.

By integrating your practice, you may come to realize every experience as a spiritual experience. So everything you do, do it with Spirit. When you walk, allow your feet to kiss the Earth. When you work, work as an act of service.

The Practical Action: *Whether you're experienced or new at this, try to extend each session of illumination you have more and more each day. Appreciation of the gift of life knows no time limits.*   - BL

Angel Rating: 1-FAT!

One for a week's practice: A fat one for a year's:

26... *grow wealth for positive purposes*

I'm not advocating being a total breadhead here, 'cause that's a fast route to losing your peace of mind and turning into an ass. But we shouldn't underestimate the power of money. Some people say money is the root of all evil, but the actual Biblical quote is: *"The love of money is the root of all evil."* This is an important distinction to make; money itself isn't evil, it's what we do with it that makes the difference. If your intentions are good, there's nothing wrong with growing money, in another aphorism, it *"makes the world go around."* Personally, I have every intention of becoming a multi-millionaire, not in order to improve my lifestyle one iota, my lifestyle's great, but in order to gain freedom to be increasingly philanthropic.

Avatar Mother Meera says, very simply: *"Everyone must work."* She gives mostly silent teachings, so if she has anything to say, it's worth a listen.

On this note let us all work hard, do a worthwhile job, and employ our disposable incomes to accumulate good deeds. Here's a financial suggestion: Given the current state of the environment, I reckon it's a good time to invest in alternative energy sources! Solar, wind, waves... Avoid ethanol. Don't quote me or sue me on this, but I say Cleantech is the way of the future!

Another thing about money here. A whole lot of the things we advocate doing in this book involve money, likely a great deal more money than you have right now. We're sorry. We know this isn't fair. There's a lot of financial inequality in the current scheme of things. Be aware that if you're reading this book, you're already one of the richest people in the world, statistically speaking.

Don't sweat the stuff you can't afford, just keep going with the other stuff, it's all good. We truly wish for you to cultivate enough grace and enough wealth to get to Heaven, and to reforest an entire African village, not necessarily in that order...

The Practical Action: *Time to stop looking under the desert ground. Look to the infinite sky. Invest at least part of your 401(k) in a mutual fund that is focused on alternative energy stocks. Analysts have forecast excellent long-term gains for "green" stocks such as solar and wind energy. Keep up on this trend and invest accordingly.*

- BL

Angel Rating: 1-FAT!

1 for a good work ethic:

A fat one for working a good business plan:

27… *don't die rich*

You can't take it with you. Really. Don't let your heirs and successors get pounded for taxes, make sure you plan your estate well in advance. If you're lucky enough to have excess cash, securities, whatever, it's a good idea to off-load it incrementally, before you get into a frail state. That way the money can go to work immediately, you may have the joy of witnessing the benefits within your lifetime, and you won't get hounded by family or Church-members when you're on your death-bed with plenty of less worldly things to think about.

I know it can take years to drum up a decent chunk of change, and you may have a certain level of attachment to it. Or if you've toiled all your life and never been able to save up a nest egg, the possibility of dying rich is purely academic. Either way, don't be afraid to die humbly. You won't need a big send-off, as you won't really be there for the funeral. As you advance in your years, it is good to grow your humility. There is no better defense against the indignities of old age than humility.

To cultivate humility, and all manner of graces, devote yourself to others. If you're retired, you're blessed to be in a position to have time for this. Your time to do good works is now. As Nelson Henderson said: *"The true meaning of life is to plant trees, under whose shade you do not expect to sit."*

- BL

Angel Rating: None! If you're reading this, you didn't die yet! Take 2 Grace Tokens for contemplating your mortality, 5 for charitable estate planning.

28... *forgive someone*

Forgive and you're free to move on. Hold onto the resentment and you're carrying around all that negative energy. Forgive and you transform a negative into a positive, as you triumph over adversity and are left all the stronger. Forgive and it may heal a rift. Or forgive, and know that forgiveness does not have to include a continuing relationship with an abuser, but may give you a clearer head to step away from them. Forgive now, because if you take it to the grave, you never know, you may have to deal with it in the afterlife.

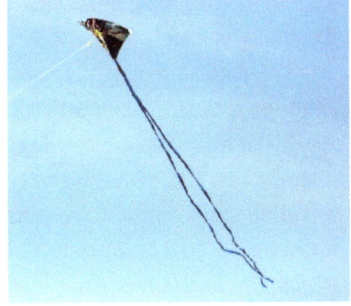

The Practical Action: *Think of the person you most need to forgive and write them a letter, explaining what they did that hurt you, and why you'd like to put it behind you. You don't have to send it. You can burn it, or tear it up and recycle it. This is an exercise to explore your feelings, in order to diminish their power over you.*

- BL

Angel Rating: 1-3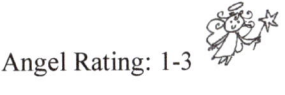

 for a co-worker or neighbor

 for an ex

 for a bad parent

29... *dispel prejudice*

To be prejudiced is to be imprisoned. Freeing someone from the tyranny of a prejudice, whether its origins be a prior experience, family, or simple ignorance, will help not only them but all they encounter. There have been times in my life when I've entered situations with preconceived notions, and they've been happily dashed. One particular time in Germany, I had just gotten off the train and was struggling to work a phone card. I knew barely any German, had never been in the country before, and assumed that Germans were for the most part stern and unhelpful and probably wouldn't be open to a young American kid asking for assistance. I was in the process of hammering the receiver into the cradle in frustration when a gentleman came up to me and offered me the use of his phonecard. It worked, and I was able to secure a hotel for the night. This gentleman and I spent a long time talking, and his parting words were ones that stuck with me: "It has been my experience that many Americans have a certain opinion of Germans, back from the World War. Now, maybe you have a different opinion. And talking with you, I now know not all Americans are 'loud Americans." This man's dispelling of my prejudice and my dispelling of his helped me shed my skin of "a stranger in a strange land," and embrace that I was a visitor in a never before seen world.

The Practical Action: *Examine your own prejudices and re-educate yourself in order to dispel them. If someone displays prejudice toward you, be aware, in your dealings with them, that you are representing whatever group or sector they are hating on, and offer them a positive experience that may help shatter their negative perceptions.*

- BP

Angel Rating: 1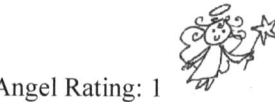

30… *look around and say "thank you"*

Gratitude doesn't go unrewarded. It may not be immediate or material, but expressing gratitude heightens one's own realization that all times have a layer of preciousness to them. By taking time out to vocally declare a thanks for existence at least once a day, we can remind ourselves of how blessed we are with the gift of life. The more we practice this, the more unconscious this thanks will become. Eventually, not only can it be  automatic to be thankful at least once a day, but then maybe once every hour, and onward from there. The swirl of life is all over the charts: from the momentous to the mundane, from excitement to tedium, and when caught up in all we go through it can be easy to lose sight of the hidden treasure of every second. But whenever one feels bored, saying "thank you" out loud to the universe is certainly an action that will focus your attention. From there, indulge yourself in thought.

The Practical Action: *Set out a time each day to practice this. It can be the first thing you do upon awakening, or it can be one of the last things you do before dropping off into sleep. Then start to vary the times. Expressing your gratitude throughout different times will help you appreciate varying situations.*

- BP

Angel Rating: 1

31... *climb a mountain, literal or metaphorical*

George Mallory, one of the first men to ever attempt climbing Mount Everest, replied when bombarded by why he would want to tackle such an intimidating task, *"Because it is there."* This is an inspiring view to take not only of a literal mountain but of any goal in our life we feel is a mountain worth climbing. When we strive for goals out of the pure joy of being able to do so, our actions are distilled with a pure sense that transcends concentration on the gain or loss of the outcome. To attempt something for the sheer thrill of tackling the challenge of doing so brings success with the very first step: "finish lines," "victories," and "losses" become irrelevant. George Mallory died on Mount Everest, and it is still a matter of contention whether or not he climbed the Second Shelf and actually made it to the top. But does it really matter? He attempted to climb Everest because it was there. We all have mountains before us. There's just one opening handhold and a pull upwards that separates us from an adventure undertaken.

The Practical Action: *If you want to run a marathon, start with a mile a day. If you've always wanted to write a novel, write the first sentence. Take the first step toward a goal.*

- BP

Angel Rating: 1

32… treat a stranger as you would your favorite animal

Most everyone has a favorite animal, the kind that when you see one you just melt. I have a friend who is absolutely in love with pitbulls. One might think this is a dangerous affection to have, but whenever he sees a strange pitbull, he approaches them. Carefully, yes, but also with tremendous love and instantaneous joy. Never once has he had a problem. Yes, this man heads over to dogs that, as a rule, are not always the most receptive to strangers, and he has never had one react with anger.

Now this is not a suggestion to go nuzzling the person next to you in the checkout line or petting a stranger on the head while cooing how cute his/her cheeks are. But a smile sure goes a long way. Like many gestures, a smile cuts across all language and culture. To share it with a stranger makes it all that much more random. And if you're the cynical type, there are practical benefits. Having worked in the service sector, I can tell you this: whenever a customer smiled at me first, I was much more inspired to go above and beyond the call of duty to help them.

The Practical Action: *Try approaching a stranger with the same openness that you would your favorite animal. Chances are it will be a pleasant encounter. If not, at the very least, they probably won't bite you.*

- BP

Angel Rating: 1

33... *remember a loved one, and do something in their honor*

Light a candle. Name a child after them. Forgive them and yourself for any misunderstandings. Attempt to accomplish something they always wanted to but never had the chance. Start a worthwhile endeavor in their name: a foundation, a scholarship, a library. Learn from their mistakes, try to understand their faults, celebrate their triumphs. Write their story.

The Practical Action: *Do anything for a loved one that will benefit not only their memory but others.*

- BP

Angel Rating: 1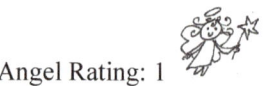

34… *feed your gratitude instead of your despair*

I have a cousin who has been paralyzed from the waist down since he was twenty years old. Yet he still has a tremendous will and has never stopped striving to be happy. Years ago when I fractured my wrist I tried to take a shower before going to the emergency room. Not having the use of my left hand was a humbling experience. After I got out of the shower I called my cousin and told him what had happened, and that I now understood about one thousandth of what he goes through a day. He laughed heartily and said I probably now understood a millionth of what he went through. The point here is that there are simple actions we do so many times throughout the day that it is easy to let the magic of them slip away. On the same token I'd venture to say that no one is ever completely happy or satisfied with what they have and that could be argued as one of the characteristics of being human. Some studies have shown that countries in Africa, while some of the most desolated, contain the least depressed people. When one is concerned about where the day's supply of water and meager meals are coming from, one has little time for philosophical wanderings. Existential angst over the meaning of life is certainly a worthwhile thing to explore, and may the day come when we all have the luxury for it. Until then, it doesn't hurt to take a timeout and leave the darkness for a while.

The Practical Action: *Should you feel yourself spiraling into despair, lie down and don't move for five minutes. When five minutes is up, be grateful you have the ability to rise and walk on.*

- BP

Angel Rating: 1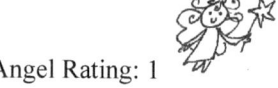

35... *eat less cows*

A lot of people think cars are the biggest source of climate changing gas. Actually it's cow burps and farts. Sheep are gassy too, but the cows are the worst. It's this big taboo thing amongst opponents of global warming, they're scared to speak out for the cows lest they look like hippies. I think that's backward, hippies are mostly harmless, actually.

Anyway, a UN report in 2006 described the meat industry as *"one of the top two or three most significant contributors to the most serious environmental problems, at every scale from local to global."*

It turns out that if you add up emissions from all the planes, boats, cars and trucks in the world, and tack on 40%, that's how much greenhouse gas the meat industry causes. Just one meat-free day a week, across America, would be equivalent to taking 8,000,000 (eight million!) cars off the road.

Reducing methane (cows' gas) also has a much faster impact than reducing petro-chemically produced CO_2; methane cycles from the atmosphere in 8 years, where CO_2 will hang around for a century. And time is of the essence when scientists predict the icecaps could be gone in the next four years.

Also, animal farming, primarily cattle ranching, has

desertified 20% of Earth's pastures, and is *"the major driver of deforestation worldwide."*

And cows aren't energy efficient. As per the USDA's Economic and Agricultural Research, it takes 16 lbs of grain to produce 1 lb of beef. Enough that 50% of grain from the third world goes to power up cows, while 24,000 people starve to death daily. One billion people suffer from hunger and malnutrition, while 1.4 billion people could be fed by the grain and soybeans eaten by US livestock.

If you can't bear to go vegetarian or vegan, know that it will help your fellow humans, your planet and your waistline if you can just skimp on the odd burger.

If you're one of those people who says they don't eat many cows, ask yourself, can you manage to eat zero cows? Zero dairy? You'd cut your impact down to zero cow fart emissions.

BTW, I'm giving this one a high Angel Rating, not because it's hard to do, it's not, it's really easy! We eat every day, and what we eat is something that we are eminently in control of. It gets Fat Angels because it has a far-reaching environmental and humanitarian effect. It may also require you to re-think, which is worth a Fat Angel. See also entries # 63, and 92 for further reading on the cows.

The Practical Action: *Don't be afraid to try a tofu steak or veggie burger. If you're not ready to kick the meat habit completely, start by cutting out one meat meal a week, and work up from there. You'll be surprised how much better you feel! Reducing one's meat intake can help not only climate change, but one's weight. Good for your health, the planet's health, and the cows' health!*

- BL

BP note: I've been a meat eater all my life, and still do enjoy the occasional Ribeye or chicken fried steak. However, I must say that a good tofu burger is not only similar in taste to a burger, but it's much less expensive. I douse it with teriyaki sauce, slap some cheese on it, and voila! For

whatever it's worth, after I cut my red meat intake down from four times a week to once a week, I lost 8 pounds in a month even though I wasn't working out any harder than usual. Plus, like many indulgences such as chocolate and martinis, red meat tends to taste even better when eaten sparingly.

Angel Rating: 1-FAT!

Cut down on beef:

Quit for a week:

A month:

A year:

A lifetime:

36... *enlarge your comfort zone*

Being comfortable with your own presence will help you to find comfort in any situation, even life-threatening ones. Living in Los Angeles, I've been accosted on the street by mentally unstable homeless people, held up at gunpoint, and had to have meetings with people who viewed me as a disposable cog in a massive machine. All of you reading have no doubt had experiences, from the mundane to the extreme, that have made you uncomfortable. It helps to remember that the larger your comfort zone is, the larger you are, and even in times of stress that means that you will be comfortable enough to enlarge your power and influence over any given situation. If you're afraid of heights, sky-dive (well worth it, I can assure you from personal experience). Or if you're paranoid about fire, always checking to make sure the stove is off before you leave the house, etc., try leaving a candle burning while you make love to your significant other. (Extremely well worth it, I can assure you from personal experience).

The Practical Action: *Feel free to take the two examples given in the text and bring the same sense of daring to a fear you may have in your own life.*

-BP

Angel Rating: 1

37... adopt a child

Here's another big taboo subject, up there with the cows: The world is overpopulated, and the planet can't breathe. There's really not enough natural resources to go around, and the rate of population increase is pushing us toward a tipping point of non-sustainability.

Personally, I admit it, I have my own child; I'm conceited about my genes, and have a terror of only the stupid people reproducing. But perfect though he is, if we were to have another child, it would be through adoption. If everyone came on board with this, population growth would be halved within a generation - and the Earth would have a chance to heal for future generations.

If you're one of those believes children are a Godsend, you are absolutely right, but see if you can open this up; God may bless you with children from outside sources, and mercifully spare you the hassles of gestation.

The Practical Action: *If you already have children and want another, open your home up to a child that needs one. If you want children but don't necessarily want a life-partner, adoption is a wonderful way for you to give a child a home and nourish yourself, your child, and the planet all at once.*

- BL

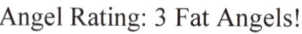

Angel Rating: 3 Fat Angels!

38... *sponsor a third world child*

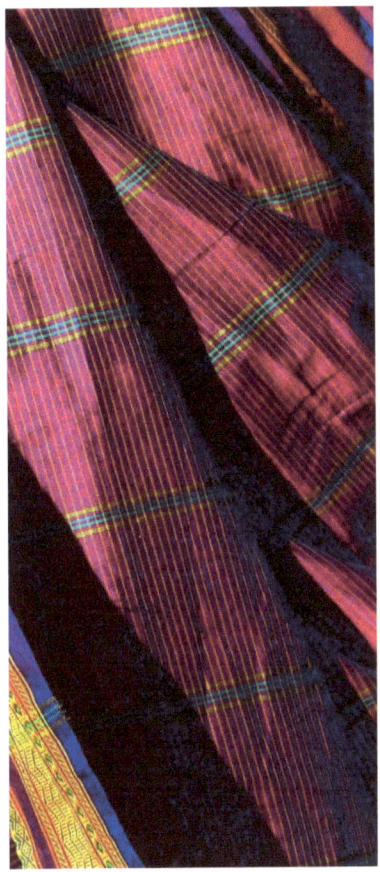

Cheaper and less labor intensive than adopting a child is sponsoring a third world child. To clarify on this, the child stays in the third world with her or his parents or guardians, and through sponsorship you get to outsource your parental responsibilities! For a monthly donation, you get the satisfaction of knowing you're providing such basics as food, shelter, medicine and education to a child who's future might otherwise be grim. Through letters and photos, you can develop a personal connection to that girl or boy, and also an insight into a culture that you might otherwise never experience.

The Practical Action: *Go to www.savethechildren.org/sponsor, www.sos-usa.org, or www.children.org. Then help as many children as you are able.*

- BL

Angel Rating: Fat Angel!

39... *be aware of what lies above and beneath.*

There is so much that is beautiful and so much that is terrible in this world. As you contemplate the spiritual, don't neglect to consider the corrupt. Awareness is awareness, and as a conscious person, it is important to grow awareness in all directions.

Some people think it's good to only contemplate the Divine, and that is all very well for the next world, but if you truly wish to realize your insignificance, I recommend contemplating this world.

History has shown that political policy can be decided according to Corporate whims. Wars can be fought over oil. Religion is often used as a weapon to divide people. The list is endless...

I recently started trading the stock market, and it was like looking into a whole new can of worms. Insider trading. Market makers forcing stocks up or down according to how they may profit. All kinds of shenanigans that I can't even begin to understand. It's hard to escape the machine, but you can be aware of what it is, what is does, and know that there are worlds within worlds within worlds, and there are worlds beyond this one.

Expand your consciousness to encompass as much as you can!

The Practical Action: *Head to www.stopcorporateabuse.org, and www.stopbigmedia.com, and throw a monkey wrench into the machine.*

- BL

Angel Rating: 2

40... *give an anonymous gift to someone you're angry at*

Why anonymous, you might ask? Because if they don't like it, at least they won't think you're trying to antagonize them further. Seriously, the act of giving a gift may serve as a reminder that if you're angry at someone it's because they're someone who you've shared plenty of life experience with. Or maybe they're a stranger who pushed a button you didn't know you had. Anger is as powerful an emotion as any, and if it rears its head, there's usually a good reason for it. So try to find the lesson, then make an anonymous first step towards amends. If possible, try to be watching unobtrusively when they receive the gift. (This works especially well for a fellow office worker). Their surprise and (hopefully) delight may remind you that they are, indeed, human.

The Practical Action: *If you have a long simmering anger at someone, perform this Way with them and release the anger along with the gift.*

- BP

Angel Rating: 1

41... *nurse a sick person – even if they have cooties*

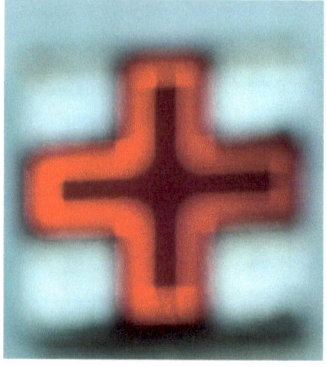

To help one who is ill – whether their ailment be physical, mental, or spiritual, whether it be AIDS or simply a case of the blues – in expressing concern for them you express concern for yourself and your role in the world. One of the signs of true love is to allow yourself to be around someone who is suffering and not be afraid of being infected. In displaying your strength you will help both them and yourself grow stronger.

The Practical Action: *If you know someone who's sick, contact them. Make a phone call. Send an email. Care for those who have cared for you.*

- BP

Angel Rating: 1

If you live with a person and nurse them through their illness, be that they recover or pass on from this world with dignity...

– FAT ANGEL!

42... *believe in a dream*

One time I asked a person who had been born blind what they dreamt about, and she smiled and gestured around, at a world she had never been able to visually see. She said: *"This. I dream this."*

Is not Heaven itself a dream? True, people believe such a paradise exists, yours truly among them. But therein lies the key, the power of belief. To believe in the dream of Heaven means one should not *act* like a good person, but *be* a good person.

So be a dreamer. Spit into the eyes of the sun. How many times when you've been woken up by the alarm clock have you been jolted out of a dream that you were enjoying? This life we have is a dream as well. Let's use it to fulfill not only others but ourselves.

Also, on a practical note, John Barrymore said that one only becomes old when regrets take the place of dreams. No one knows for certain what awaits us when we pass from this world, but if one doesn't believe in a dream of a better place, chances are it will be much harder to recognize a pathway to one.

The Practical Action: *Think back on your life and note any regrets. Then think of a dream you can follow that will eliminate the regret. If you regret never becoming a professional baseball player, volunteer to coach a little league team and help others achieve their dreams. Both of you will win.*

- BP

Angel Rating: 1

43... *dream big*

If you set your sights high, you may not achieve all your goals, but you'll probably get further than if you aimed low. It's important to set clear objectives. Think about how you would like to have benefited the world a year from now, five years, ten, what you'd like on your epitaph. Make up a list of simple little steps to achieve this, and stick to the plan. Don't get too hung up on failure. The most successful people are actually the ones who have dared to fail most often.

Look at Abraham Lincoln, he had two failed businesses, a nervous breakdown and seven defeats for political office, but it didn't stop him from becoming President!

- BL

The Practical Action: *Do something far-reaching and good. Start today. As Goethe said: "Whatever you can do, or dream you can, begin it. Boldness has genius, power and magic to it."*

Angel Rating: 1

44a... *help a stray animal to a no-kill rescue center*

First, of course, check to make sure they have no tags or chips. Then, if you don't have the necessary facilities to house them for a few days while you paper the neighborhood with "PET FOUND" posters, head over to www.saveourstrays.com and locate a no-kill rescue center. And also, if you DO happen to have the

necessary facilities to house a pet, consider adopting one. Buying an animal that is "pure bred" is all well and good, but to rescue another being and give it a home is not just less expensive; it is priceless.

- BP

And as Blaze can attest to the joys of:

44b... *rescue an animal*

Sometimes they rescue you, too. Sometimes it's like you're meant to be together.

I was so lonely when I first came to L.A., I wished for just a small, stripy cat I could call Friend. I didn't mention this to anyone. A few days later, my neighbor came over, saying, "I have something for you." He took Friend out of his pocket. She was exactly as I had imagined, very stripy and very naughty. She'd been running wild in the garden of a crack-house. My neighbor had chased down all of her sisters and brothers and found them homes, and Friend was the elusive last one.

After I got Friend, things picked up a bit for me, and I met some new people. One of them brought his pet boa constrictor to stay while he was moving apartments. Friend went and sat beside the snake's tank all day, as the snake gazed hungrily back. It was then that I realized Friend needed a friend.

I found Stuff in a pound in South Central, small, scruffy and flea-ridden. He was stripy too, and had somehow lost his mom. The moment I saw him, he cried to be rescued. Friend immediately adopted him as her kitten. Emotionally, he's never grown up; he's still a nervous eater and terribly sensitive. But he's the sweetest, most affectionate cat ever.

A while later, I met a wonderful guy with two rescued tuxedo cats, we got married, and our cat colony was complete. Our house has become the envy of several of the neighborhood cats. They stare longingly through our patio doors, wanting to join the party. If they don't have a good home we will find them one. If we go visit later, they will run up and meow about how grateful they are. Our cats are all great cats. We're very lucky to have them. It's hard to imagine them ever being without homes.

The Practical Action: *Don't let the next stray animal you see pass you by. Also, please don't ever bring an animal to an animal shelter that executes animals that don't get adopted. If you are going to adopt an animal, do so from an animal shelter, not a breeder.*

- BL

Angel Rating: 2

45... *go carbon neutral*

Tibetan tulku Sogyal Rinpoche says, *"If you can't do good, at least try not to do harm."* Sage advice, but actually harder than it might seem once you really start thinking about it.

Okay, so you've Greened your life, reduced your carbon footprint, and passed the message on to your adopted child. You've replaced all your bulbs with CFLs, turned down your thermostat, inflated your tires, you carry a cup around with you so's not to generate waste with your lattes. There's still little things nagging at your conscience. You just painted the wall with VOC-free paint. You're still trying to save up for that solar paneling. Friends may think you're worrying too much, but you know you've every right to be concerned. It's time to go carbon neutral.

Going carbon neutral is when you go the extra mile to make up for those pesky CO2 emissions you just can't seem to shake. Actually, you can do this at any stage of your Greening efforts, but it'll just cost you more if you aren't going Green in other ways. By offsetting bad environmental karmas with good ones, you reduce your environmental impact to zero. You can do this on your own by planting a bunch of trees or whatever you 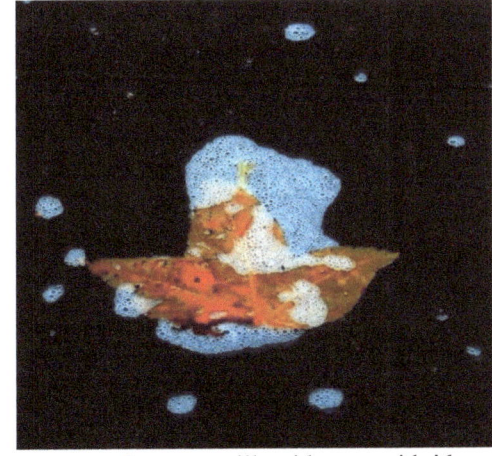 want, www.countdownyourcarbon.org will guide you with ideas. There's also websites where you can calculate your net emissions for the year and then purchase carbon offsets that fund various types of Greening projects. It's not as expensive as you would think, either. Check out: www.carbonfund.org, www.terrapass.com and www.self.org (SELF is an acronym for Solar Electric Light Fund.)

BP note: And for all you scoundrels out there, check out www.cheatneutral.com. It's a great way to come clean and save the planet in one fell swoop.

The Practical Action: *Start a contest with a group of your friends in regards to all of you reducing your respective carbon footprints. Have prizes for the greatest reduction, the shortest amount of time, the most creative ways, and the like. Then throw a party and celebrate with cocktails in recyclable cups and all-natural cookies.*

- BL

Angel Rating: 1

46... *throw a joke instead of an insult*

True, Sigmund Freud was fond of some wild theories about mothers, not to mention various substances. But he did point out that "the first human who hurled an insult instead of a stone was the founder of civilization." Well, to go Freud one better, the first person who hurled a humorous barb instead of a malicious one was the founder of elevated consciousness. Laughter is the key to one's heart, and once you are admitted to one's heart, you can find your way into their mind as well. This will help not only with a nasty boss or co-worker but with more intimate relationships as well. Guys, we all know that if you can make a beautiful woman laugh, you score major points. So everyone, feel free to make as many jokes throughout the day as you want. Remember, jokes are like pizza; even if they're a tad on the cheesy side, they're still pretty good. And if confronted with a situation that could escalate into physical violence, you'll be ready with a very powerful weapon: humor. If you don't believe me, remember Richard Pryor, who claimed he made people laugh all day long in jail to avoid, um, unpleasant consequences.

Laughter. Use it.

The Practical Action: *The next time you feel like expressing your anger at someone, do so. But tell them a joke first. Laughter has a way of cutting anger down to a size where you can reason with it.*

- BP

Angel Rating: 1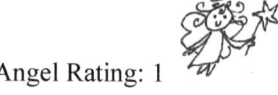

47... *question your intolerance of others*

Given enough time and fuel, intolerance boils over into violence and terror. The key to toppling intolerance is to ask a simply complex question: "Why?" Growing up, I was raised in an extremely homophobic household. When I left home as a young adult, I was of the opinion homosexuals were evil and should be shunned. Of course, I had never really met any people who I knew to be homosexual. Later in my life, when I did meet a person who I became friends with and months after we'd been friends found out he was gay, my feelings were turned upside down. Could it be possible, I asked myself, that I was being intolerant simply because of my own ignorance? The answer I came up with (though admittedly it took me quite a while) was a resounding yes. The tricky thing about slaying intolerance is that sometimes we must slay part of ourselves, how we were raised, or even the opinions of those we've looked up to. I speak from experience when I say it's not easy, but given the alternative of people hating one another, fighting one another, and blowing themselves up, questioning one's self and one's intolerance is definitely a worthy task.

The Practical Action: *The next time you find yourself hating something or someone, ask yourself why this is. If you feel someone's difference makes them wrong and amoral, do some research into why they are the way they are. If you still feel they are wrong, forgive them and move on. Don't spend your energy on blind hatred.*

- BP

Angel Rating: 1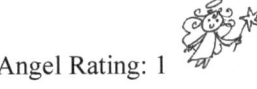

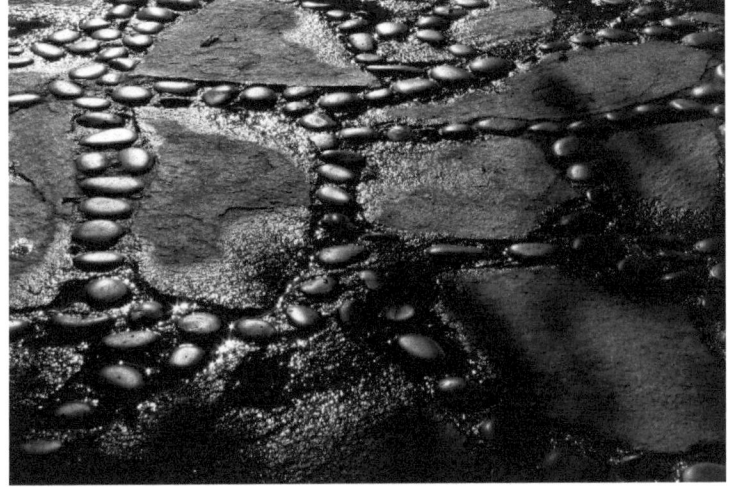

48... *stitch up someone's stuffed animal*

Stuffed animals bring out the child in all of us. One of the wondrous things about being a child is the fearlessness that youth nurtures. To help repair a person's stuffed animal is to restore that person's child within. There are people well into their eighties who still have and cherish stuffed animals they were given in their youth. But though stuffed animals are precious they, like humans, do age. To doctor another's stuffed animal is to be a protector of the child within that person.

The Practical Action: *If you see someone's stuffed animal is looking a bit worse for wear, and if you can sew, offer to perform "stuffed animal surgery." If you can't sew, learn. You never know when you might need it!*

- BP

Angel Rating: 1

49... *document another's life*

This works best if you start when the person whose life you're chronicling is a child (i.e. a grandchild, niece or nephew). Keep pictures of them as they grow. If they send you cards or projects from school, preserve them. It's so easy to forget about events or stages in one's childhood; pictures and mementos from different periods in our lives can unlock treasure troves of memories. It's often said that the energy of youth is wasted on the young; this may be true, because when we're young we have all the time in the world (at least it may feel that way). So when we're young we don't necessarily take the time to capture moments and really appreciate individual memories. However, looking back on one's youth can be amazing in that it shows how much has been learned, how many mistakes (both stupid and wonderful) have been made, and how long a journey it's been. Help a loved one navigate their past by keeping a photo album, a collection of their letters, and any kind of possessions from their childhood. I'll always be grateful to my Uncle Larry and his family for letting me store a few trunks from my childhood home in their attic. When I looked through them recently, I found they contained old comic books, pictures, school papers... even my Batman and Joker action figures.

It was as if I'd found a uniquely precious buried treasure, a time capsule of sorts. It was wonderful to spend time leafing through my past. So often, feelings that seem so fleeting back when we're young prove to be more resilient than many material objects.

The Practical Action: *Preserve another's life in some way. Be it through pictures, writings, or other ways. Offer to store their possessions when they move away for college or to start a new chapter in their lives. Down the road, they may want to revisit previous chapters in their life, like rereading a book with a new perspective.*

- BP

Angel Rating: 1

50... *hug someone, even if it's yourself*

Touch is the most basic form of communication. It is essential to human health and well-being. Without it, babies will fail to thrive. (If you have issues with your parents, it may help to remember that however awful they are, the likelihood is they did once hold you lovingly, or you wouldn't have survived.)

Touching and hugging is a way to reach out to others that goes beyond words. Therapeutic hugs are all about friendship, healing, and love. Ask first if unsure that the recipient is open to your hug, and don't confuse a platonic hug with a sexual advance. If you've had a bad day and there's no one else around, give yourself a hug, you deserve it! But of course, hugs work best with two people. Hugs are good for self-esteem for both parties. Don't ever think you have nothing to give when you still have your open arms.

Kathleen Keating's *"The Little Book of Hugs,"* which is really cute and well worth a read, suggests we *"Hug often. Hug well."*

BP Note: As a guy who can sometimes be very affectionate for any number of reasons, ranging from if the Cubs ever win a World Series to every time a touchdown is scored in a football game, it saddens me that the sight of two guys hugging can provoke homophobic reactions. Actually homophobia is just sad, period. (See Way #47) So everyone loosen up and give people hugs with no strings attached!

The Practical Action: *Hug someone whenever it's appropriate! If you really want to go big with this, organize a "Free Hug" event. This is where people write signs that say "FREE HUGS," then gather in a busy area such as a concert or a tourist attraction. They then disperse into the crowd and hug whoever is open to the action.*

- BL

Angel Rating: 1-2

 for hugging someone

 for organizing a "Free Hugs" Event

51... *don't ever become too powerful to look up to another*

How boring life would be if there were no challenges left! To always have someone else to look up to insures not only a healthy dose of humility (which is a much more attractive feature than arrogance) but also will keep one always inspired. Whatever your gift may be, there is always the possibility for growth. To admire someone else's talent, or aspects of the same talent you may have, means that there is another step for you to climb. Have the wisdom to admire someone else's skill, compliment them on it, for this will fuel not only them but yourself.

The Practical Action: Pay someone an honest compliment.

- BP

Angel Rating: 1

52... ride a bicycle at least once a week

Not only does this not produce pollution, it increases health. Also, you will notice more on a bicycle. If you see a person you find attractive, it'll be easier to stop and talk to them and impress them with how ecologically conscious you are. And when was the last time a bicyclist went through "road rage?" It's also sometimes very practical to bike. When you crave a bottle of chocolate milk and a bag of potato chips at eleven fifteen at night, you can bike to the all-night corner store and know that at least you're burning off some of those high octane delicious calories you're going to soon be consuming.

The Practical Action: *Use your bike not only for practical activities, but also take your weekly ride through an area outside of your immediate neighborhood which you've never explored before.*

- BP

Angel Rating: 1

53… *appreciate your smallness in the depth of infinity*

Every now and then it does a spirit good to get out of the bustle of everyday life and realize how much power we as human beings have to *"make mountains out of molehills."* Travel out into the desert, or the beach, or any place away from the glare of manmade lights and look up to the night sky and observe the lightshow of this galaxy. Its constellations and shooting stars rival any special effects production. Not only does one get the visual enjoyment, but the solitude is a good reminder that we as individuals are miniscule in all that the universe sees. Our problems are real, yes. Our disappointments and triumphs often occupy the center of our world. But when one ponders how we are but one collection of atoms on one planet out of an infinite collection of worlds, it helps to bring things into perspective, and can lend peace in times of despair. Also this can make us realize just how many others we are sharing this existence with.

The Practical Action: *Spend the night under a spray of stars away from familiar surroundings. Take this opportunity to stare at the sky and allow your consciousness to join its map of potentiality.*

- BP

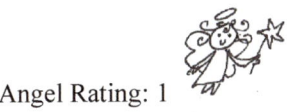

Angel Rating: 1

54... *consider your impact within the space of one lifetime*

You don't have to be the ruler of a country, a scientist, or a rock star to make a difference in people's lives. In reality, the vast majority of our lives don't make the five o'clock news or get headlines in newspapers. But that doesn't mean our experiences are any less worthy, and it also doesn't negate the impact we can have on another's life. Teachers aren't rock stars, but almost everyone I know can remember a teacher who inspired them at one point in their life. Then there are those who are seemingly random; Marvin was a man who worked at my grandfather's jewelry shop and would always ask me, *"Ben, how's the writing going?"* Even through my high school years when I'd temporarily shelved writing in favor of more important things, like being a teenager. Now, when I'm writing, I'll find myself saying with a smile, *"Marvin, it's going pretty good."* We all have a shared superpower, and that is the ability to make a difference in another's life. Now it's up to us to choose how we want to use our superpower. Superman or Lex Luthor: try and guess which one's the frontrunner for getting into Heaven.

The Practical Action: *After spending a night staring at the stars, take the next day to throw a positive pebble into the ocean of infinity by making a positive difference in at least one person's life.*

- BP

Angel Rating: 1

55... *learn about a religion different than your own*

It's a big old world out there. I think it's odd that religion, the source of most people's spiritual sustenance, is also a big cause of division between people. It's kind of missing the point.

If you ever catch yourself in an attitude of, "I am right, you are wrong," ask questions. It is likely that you will find common ground somewhere with the other party. As it turns out, all of the major religions intersect in some way on the most important points. This might seem blasphemous, but tolerance is a good thing all around. Loving thy neighbor, and all that.

The Practical Action: *To see 5000 years of religion mapped out in 90 seconds, complete with details of the larger religious conflicts, go to:*

http://www.mapsofwar.com/ind/history-of-religion.html

- BL

Angel Rating: 1

56... *tell a child you love them*

I have to tell my kid I love him at least three times a day – he's so darned cute! I'm only including it here cause I hear it can be hard for some people. People, don't be afraid to speak your love! Whoever it's for! Just don't piss anyone off!

Let it fly, chances are it will come back to you!

I also mention the child thing cause there's a lot about parenting – if you do it right - that's worthy of a ticket to Heaven. My son's godfather, Thane, has three children and infinite patience. I don't know if he was born with such grace, or cultivated it as a survival skill, but regardless, I am proud to know him.

BP note: Not to complain, but I wish Blaze had been my mom.

BL note: You are complaining. And it's just creepy! ;)

***The Practical Action:** Kids who have love vocally demonstrated to them are much more likely to grow into adults who aren't afraid to vocally demonstrate their love to* their *children, and so on. So be another link in a chain of love!*

- BL

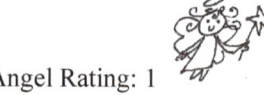

Angel Rating: 1

57... *kiss a polar bear*

Of course, I don't actually mean "kiss a polar bear," you'd have to go a long way, and then it would bite. But I worry about the polar bears. Just seeing one on one of those BBC shows is enough to make me cry! Yes, polar bears are becoming increasingly rare. The ice caps are melting at such a rate that they're drowning trying to swim to the next iceberg. Their snow dens are collapsing and smothering the cubs. If the mothers' fat reserves fall much further, they will be unable to reproduce at all. So I worry about the polar bears, and the penguins, and the ice caps, and in fact, Heaven help us all.

Senator John Edwards describes the polar situation thus: *"If you leave a piece of white cardboard out, it will reflect the sun and won't get too hot. If you leave a piece of black cardboard out, it will soak up the sun and heat up fast. If the ice caps melt, the sun will be shining into black ocean depths, and global warming will only accelerate."*

Polar bears are not only cute and cuddly looking, they are a symbol of the many things we stand to lose in the climate crisis. By lobbying to get them on the official endangered species list, we acknowledge that we must take direct action on behalf of the animals to prevent global warming.

The Practical Action: *Check out the Natural Resources Development Council: www.nrdc.org. On this site you can get involved with lobbying action on behalf of polar bears. You can also adopt a polar bear, penguin, or other endangered animal through donation at: www.wildlifeadoption.org. Polar bears can make great wedding gifts! They'll send the happy couple a certificate of adoption, and a stuffed polar bear, or a brace of stuffed polar bears! It's a great way to embark upon married life!* - BL

Angel Rating: 1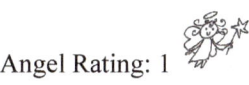

58... *seek the highest good in any situation*

Whatever you do, just seek the highest good. Some situations can be confusing. Go to your center and meditate on what the highest good is. Your heart will tell you. Once you've got this straight, life will be so much easier!

The highest good means considering the needs of others, but does not mean you have to sacrifice yourself all the time. If you take yourself out of the picture, you may disempower yourself from coming back to do good another day. As a force for good in the world, you are part of the overall equation.

Sometimes you may find yourself drawn towards a controversial decision. That is okay, so long as your decision is directed towards the highest good.

Also, if your mind is clouded by attachments, be willing to defer judgment. I've a friend who's big on praying, but also quite a materialist. I find this annoying at times, but to her credit, whenever she prays, she puts in her requests with the caveat "for the highest good of all concerned." I guess this minimizes the impact of misguided prayer requests.

The Practical Action: *Think of the last time you made a decision you weren't altogether certain was the right thing to do. Go back and analyze whether or not it was for the highest good, or for more selfish reasons. Learn from it, and the next time you are faced with a challenging decision, take the time to think* *through your options and map out which of them would be most suited to the highest good. Don't be afraid to make an unpopular decision if you feel in your hearth that the highest good will be served as a result.*

- BL

Angel Rating: 2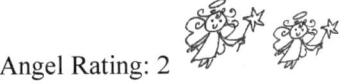

59... *let a person younger than yourself know that they're cool*

It doesn't matter the age difference. People of all ages like approval, and there are certain times in one's life where this approval is key. You can be a wicked Uncle, a mellow cousin, an eccentric grandmother, a good friend... what matters most is letting a younger person who may be dealing with a situation know that you've been there, you've survived, and that they will, too. Broken hearts and disappointments are part of life. But if you've gone through them, allow someone the benefit of your experience and support. I've advised nephews in the role of a wicked uncle, and also been the recipient of advice from one of *my* wicked uncles, who told me, "Ben we don't get smarter as we get older. We just get less stupid." This was proposed to me after I'd just hinted about dropping out of college to move to Tennessee, where I planned to follow a childhood dream and become a professional wrestler and make thirty dollars a night. My uncle assured me he'd be behind me. I could almost see his grimace through the phone, but his words were strong and true. He was telling me, I suppose, that I was still cool, even if I made disastrous choices. That he didn't lecture me and automatically tell me I was being foolish made me look long and hard at my choices instead of automatically defying "authority." I wound up staying in college and graduating. I also became a professional wrestler, but at least I was less stupid when I did so. There's another Way to get into Heaven by treating older people as People and not "old people." The same rings true with the young.

The Practical Action: *If there's a young person in your life, stand behind them even if you think they're crazy. Chances are an older person in your life once felt the same about you.*

- BP

Angel Rating: 1

60... *learn sign language*

For those of you who have trouble with auditory foreign languages, consider learning how to sign. Not only does signing open up your interaction with the hearing impaired, but also makes one appreciate how imperative the need for communication is, and how adept animals are at attaining that communication over so many different challenges. Yes, I said animals. Signing isn't just for human beings. Should you be in the Washington area and not getting much communication from Congress, try heading for the Central University, where you may get better conversation from the group of chimpanzees who live there.

Details on "Chimposiums" @ www.friendsofwashoe.org.

The project was the first to teach animals a human language. The group's matriarch, Washoe, learned 250 signs before her recent death. Blaze is friends with the son of the scientists who taught her; he actually grew up with the chimp family. In Washoe's eulogy he described her as "An enlightened being who came here to teach us."

The Practical Action: *The universal "one finger salute" is, quite frankly, pretty much known to all across the world. Well, let's start another universal trend. Learn a POSITIVE non-verbal sign. Something along the order of "God Bless" or "I love you." Then keep adding phrases from there, day by day, week by week.*

- BP

Angel Rating: 2

61... *if a work of art affects you profoundly, write the creator*

Creating a work of art can be exhilarating; it can also be torturous. *The Agony and the Ecstasy* deals with Michelangelo's painting of the Sistine Chapel. Even the conception of such an enduring masterpiece was fraught with challenges, frustrations, and sometimes plain old misery. Creation can be a long, strange, difficult trip. But a worthy one. An artist is someone who is letting you into their hearts, and is being courageous enough to feel they can help change you by  filling a blank space with a piece of themselves. That act is admirable, but so is spending the time and patience to examine said act. As has been said, *"those who are able to read and choose not to are more ignorant than those who are unable to."* This extends to all works of art, not just books. There's a well-known saying that proposes if a tree falls and nobody hears it, did it really fall? Think of an artist as someone who's *growing* a tree in a forest. You as an appreciator of art are an explorer hiking down a trail. Your eyes fall on a tree, and its appearance makes you view life in a slightly different way, for good or ill. Whether you think an artist's work is a grand achievement or an abomination, if it affects you, let them know you glimpsed their creation. Artists and those who are affected by their art can both learn from one another.

The Practical Action: *What are you waiting for? Send us a letter! Just kidding. Do this with any work of art that has made a* *difference in the way you view the world.*

- BP

Angel Rating: 1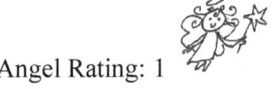

62... *vote for something*

If you are fortunate enough to have the power to make your voice heard, by all means use it. Throughout history, people around the world have given their lives for this right. From as far back as Spartacus leading Roman slaves in 72 B.C., the will of oppressed people standing up for their right to be heard cuts across all corners of the globe. The revolution that has impacted my life the most is, of course, The American Revolution. It's one thing to learn about it in History class in school, it's quite another to see Democracy in action. Lately there's been a lot of noise made about "the youth vote." Well, in 2004, only 46 percent of registered voters who were 18-24 years old bothered to vote. That's less than half of eligible voters! 24-35 year olds weren't much better, with 55 percent bothering to go to the polling booths. More people voted for the 2006 winner of American Idol than bothered to cast a vote in the 2004 Presidential Election. This is alarming. It doesn't matter if you want change or you want to keep things the way they are. VOTE! To ignore your power to vote is to display a terrible apathy. If politics disgust you, join the club. However, there are ways to change things. Vote for a write-in candidate, vote for a third-party candidate, or even write on your ballot "I PROTEST THIS FRAUD." But do vote. Do honor those who have sacrificed themselves for you. By not voting, you don't express disgust; you express apathy. If you're of the opinion of saying "screw the system," you're wrong. If you don't vote, you give "the system" the opportunity to screw you. The only thing you're screwing over by choosing not to vote is the memory of those who gave their lives for you to have a power you choose not to exercise.

The Practical Action: If you're not registered to vote, then register! Educate yourself about the candidates and issues, then vote accordingly. If there's no election coming up, you can get an angel by boycotting reality T.V. for a month.

- BP

Angel Rating: 1

63... *respect your fellow earthlings*

We are a nation of animal lovers. We lavish all kinds of love and money and apparel on our pets. Yet at many levels, our society believes that animals are there purely for our benefit.

The documentary *"Earthling"* examines our attitudes

toward our "non-human providers" and contends that *"If a being suffers, there can be no moral justification for that suffering."*

Undoubtedly animals suffer, but people draw the line in different places as to what levels of suffering are acceptable, so an important thing here is to think through what's acceptable to you. What would be arrest-worthy offenses if inflicted on dogs or cats are routinely perpetrated on farm animals and lab animals. Is it okay for an animal to suffer –

For the marketing of a cosmetic or household or product?

So that yet another drug or tobacco product can be labeled "safe" under an improper science?

Because its coat will look good on you?

Because you like the way it tastes?

The issues are way too complex to go into here, if you're interested, go to www.peta.org. It is up to you to decide where you stand on this, and what, accordingly, are consumer choices that reflect that stance. The power is within you, so stay strong and be as informed as possible.

Just as attitudes of sexism and racism have become increasingly unpopular, it is my hope that speciesism will one day fall from favor.

- BL

Angel Rating: 3

BP Note: Even though speciesism may or may not be an actual word, I couldn't agree more, and on that note…

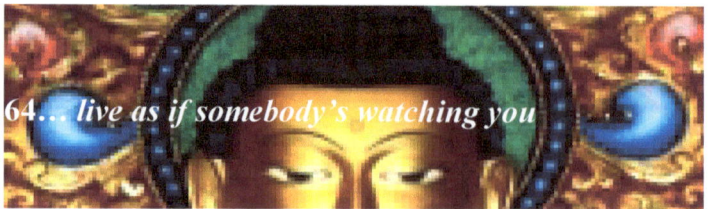

64... live as if somebody's watching you

      There is a keen possibility that other life forms exist in this universe, and if we ever do encounter them we should keep in mind that they will hopefully try and come in peace. However, the Durant Brothers made a point in their book *"Lessons of History,"* when they stated that the only hope for the people of Earth to come together in peace is if we went to war with another planet. Well, maybe we should imagine there are aliens out there waiting to devour us, and act to put aside our own differences and stand together. Then, if we ever become engaged with a hostile alien species, we'll be ready. At the very least, we'll be getting along and celebrating how our differences can unite us rather than divide us.

The Practical Action: *The next time you're tempted to do something obnoxious, keep in mind that some higher intelligence could be watching. Let whatever force you may imagine this to be know that you're doing your best by not doing the obnoxious thing.*

- BP

Angel Rating: 1

65... *be really good at just one thing*

I've had the good fortune, a couple of times, to meet Savion Glover, the world's premier tap dancer. The first time I saw him was onstage at Royce Hall, tapping to classical music. We were only a few minutes into the performance when I realized what he was doing was completely impossible. He excelled to levels beyond all comprehension. What he achieved was physically impossible. And then he kept on doing it for two hours straight, pausing only to change his shirt, which was soaked to the cuffs. What he achieved was mentally impossible. He tapped all the way through the Vivaldi's *"Four Seasons,"* some Bach, Mozart, Mendelssohn, Dvorak, Bartok and a bunch of extemporized stuff that I was amazed a classical orchestra would be down with. It didn't take long to realize, we were in the presence of the veritable Buddha of tap. He didn't miss a beat. His focus was unwavering, incredible. His heels popped like firecrackers, and he was having a blast!

Afterward we went backstage, and his aura was spread so wide I could see it glowing ten feet away. Just shaking his hand carried an immense energetic charge. He had completely transported himself to a higher plane of existence. High enough to buoy his audience up with him.

It is a common phenomena amongst artists, that they experience fugue states in which everything flows. For Savion, everything is music, everything is movement. In fugue, your mind clears of all else but the art. The art becomes the meditation. The meditation is a gateway to realize the impossible.

I can't tell you what you're good at, but whatever it is, it's worth giving it your best shot. Be really good at one thing. You never know what you might accomplish.

The Practical Action: *Figure out one thing you'd like to be really good at, and go do that thing. It needn't be lofty, and you don't need to excel beyond other people's standards, just your* *own. Pick something you love, because your plan is to practice at it for a very long time!*

- BL

Angel Rating: 4

This one gets a high rating, as it can take years to perfect your craft!

66… *take pride in what you do*

I haven't met too many people who are "world premier" at anything. However, I have met bus drivers, janitors, teachers, and many other unsung heroes of this world. Everyone has a role in helping make this reality happen, and as John Updike has said, *"Any activity becomes creative when the doer cares about doing it better."* Having worked many "day jobs," I'm familiar with the obscure pride that can come in getting a railing polished to a pristine shine, or having a customer in a checkout line compliment your efficiency. Every act is a potential art form, and whatever you may aspire to, enjoying your current activity as a creative endeavor is a strong way to get there.

The Practical Action: *Spend a day celebrating your mundane actions. Make brushing your teeth in the morning a symphony, and go from there.*

- BP

Angel Rating: 1

67... *retain your innocence*

The next time I saw Savion was at the Hollywood Bowl. We took our son backstage, clutching a *"Happy Feet"* DVD. Xai really had little sense of who Savion was, being only six years old, but was impressed to know that he was the dancer behind the penguin feet. Savion shook his hand and asked if he could see some moves. Xai broke into a spontaneous burst of stomping. It wasn't the most polished or coordinated thing, but Savion and everyone loved it! One of the many things that amazes me about Xai is that he has such trust, that he can get out there and try new things, without censoring himself. There is a great deal of power in such an attitude.

As adults, we try not to be naive, but there's a lot to be said for innocence. When you put yourself out there, offer up a belief it will be perfect and that you will be loved. Believe it, and for the most part, things work out exactly that way.

The Practical Action: *To regain a sense of innocence, spend time with children. Read them stories. Children's stories are simplistic and hopeful. How cool is that?!*

- BL

Angel Rating: 1

68... *massage a blade of grass*

So often people may take grass for granted, but the truth is not only does grass make a front lawn look great, but it plays an integral part in the environment. The front lawns of eight average houses have the same cooling effect as twenty-four home central air conditioning units. When grass absorbs rainfall, its root mass and soil microbes act as filters to capture and break down pollutants. At the same time, grass releases oxygen and absorbs carbon dioxide. Henry David Thoreau wrote about how a person who spends an afternoon in the woods truly appreciating nature is in danger of being called a loafer, while the one who contemplates a strategy on how to cut the forest down and "masking earth bald before her time" is called an enterpriser. Don't be afraid to be a loafer. Stretch out on a patch of grass and truly enjoy this planet we've been blessed with.

The Practical Action: *Realize that even a blade of grass has a full lifetime inside of it. Then carry that appreciation on to all of nature, including your fellow beings.*

- BP

Angel Rating: 1

69... *live longer by devoting your life*

A lot of the entries in this book involve volunteering, and so I'd just like to say something general about volunteering here. Volunteering and activism are great, because they benefit others and change the world. I hope you all do it out of the good of your heart. This book is all about fostering altruism. But there's also a compelling argument for doing it for selfish reasons! Studies have shown that good deeds are actually good *for* your heart. They elevate mood, improve physical health, and actually prolong life expectancy! According to *The Buck Institute for Age Research,* older volunteers have a 44% decreased mortality rate, with volunteers for more than one organization experiencing a 63% decrease! Volunteering keeps you engaged with life by taking you out of yourself. If you lose something or someone you care about deeply, volunteering to help others, perhaps others in the same boat as yourself, will help you get through the grief faster.

It's important to declare your passion and stand in your power. Opportunities for activism abound!

The Practical Action: *If you're already going to the gym a fair amount, take a day off and use that time to be of service to* *others. If you're not currently working out regularly, start volunteering regularly. For daily ideas for actions, check out www.365act.com. If you like what you experience, there are regular ongoing volunteer opportunities matched by zip at: www.volunteermatch.org.*

- BL

Angel Rating: 1-FAT, dependent on your level of volunteerism.

70... *give a piece of handmade art to someone*

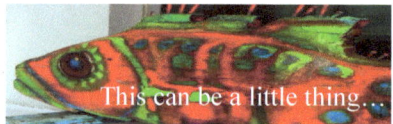

Or it could be a huge, extravagant thing, if you've a hidden masterpiece in you.

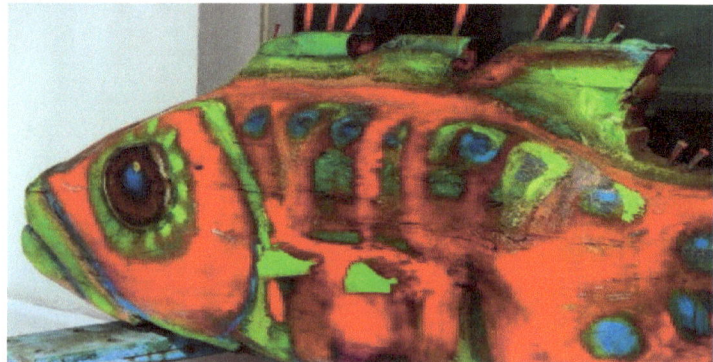

This is about showing someone you care. It's also very satisfying to work with your hands. There's a lot of humility in it. Jesus was a carpenter, and so was Harrison Ford, and look how they turned out.

If you're not handy, it doesn't have to be your own original, you could use someone else's. If you have children, their sticky hands create the very best handmade art, and it's fun to make some with them.

The Practical Action: *Instead of giving flowers or a Hallmark Card, give a piece of art instead. Or if you're going to a party, bring a piece of art instead of a bottle of wine.*

- BL

Angel Rating: 1

71… *learn CPR*

You can get certified at your local adult school. You never know when it might come in handy. Heaven forfend, but children choke on buttons, adults keel over from stress. While you're at it, learn the Heimlich maneuver too. This is one of those good karmas that you hope you never need, but it's really worth knowing, cause it's the chance to save a life.

The Practical Action: *Once you've learned CPR, pray you never have to use it.* ;)

- BL

Angel Rating: 2

72... *laugh easily*

Don't take it all too seriously! Laughter is a good stress reliever, raises endorphins, and is beneficial to health. A Good Sense Of Humor will score you points on most dating websites. It can both break the ice at parties and break up potential fights. All kinds of differences can be swept aside by the simple sound of a child's laughter. There's a universality to it that can bridge any language gap. The next time someone cuts you off on the freeway, or is snappish, try and remember that they most likely take simple joy in something we ALL share: the power of laughter.

For more information on laughter therapy, head to www.laughtertherapy.com

The Practical Action: *Think of one thing about yourself that makes you laugh. Then laugh out loud at yourself. If you can't think of anything, try to recall the kind of clothes you wore in high school. Having grown up in the 1980s, this does the trick for me every time. Also, memorize a good joke to have in your repertoire should the need for one arise.*

- BP

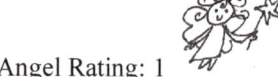

Angel Rating: 1

73... *give the gift of good will for the holidays*

This is a really cool one. Go to www.seva.org. They're great! They have programs in countries where people don't have access to medical care. (Even worse than in the U.S....) You can restore sight to the blind, train a midwife, health screen a child, all for nominal fees and in honor of a friend or relative. The honoree will be sent a card informing them that you donated in their name, and with a message of your choice. This is good karma all around. It's good for the gift recipient, it's good for the people who benefit from your donations, and yes, it's even good for you, too!

A funny side-note on this one is, it's somehow a gauge of where the recipient's head's at. Some people will be over-the-moon gushing grateful, others will not appreciate it much. Do not neglect these latter people. They need it most of all. Just maybe get them a little small something that they can unwrap, too. And keep a secret smile, in the knowledge that somewhere in the Himalayas, a cataract victim is able to look upon their yak again, and will always keep praying for your ingrate friend.

There's also www.networkforgood.org, and www.justgive.org, which are overview sites that will connect you with charities that have donate and give programs - but Seva is my personal favorite.

The Practical Action: *This holiday season, give a gift to someone that helps others. This way, both you and the recipient will know that you are helping others. Such a gift is not only priceless, it's eternal. Not to mention it won't be placed in an attic only to be re-gifted next holiday season.*

- BL

Angel Rating: 2

74... *stress more or less*

This one falls into the category of, "If you want to help other people, you must first help yourself." Your stress level may be fine, in which case, just work on cultivating your peace. If not, know this: It is important to find a good, healthy level of stress, where you feel energized, motivated and useful.

A lot of people will tell you not to stress, but I think it's nice to stress just enough that you can engage fully. In the decade or so that I worked as a shiatsu therapist, I was struck not only by how stressed half my clients were they came in, but also by how under-stressed the other half were. Make no mistake, under-stress is a killer. Stress is easy to identify, stressful jobs include dentist, teacher, attorney, anything that involves a potentially hostile environment and heavy workload. Under-stressful jobs include factory work, typing, answering phones; anything that seems pointless, repetitious, and underpaid. Yes, parenting can fall into this category if you don't get a break. It's the feeling of being disempowered and underappreciated that gets to people. Under-stress will get you sick just as fast as over-stress.

If you're over-or-under-stressed, examine where it's coming from. If it's external stuff, see what can be changed. You may be able to change or re-evaluate your work or your relationships or your home environment. Whatever you can't change, see if there's ways you can become more accepting and less hassled by it. Bear in mind that some people can function under very high levels of pressure without suffering any ill effects. This may be because they feel they're doing something worthwhile, and so they don't worry about what they have to endure in order to achieve it. Some people enjoy that feeling of rising to a challenge. I do!

Sometimes you don't need to quit your job or change your lifestyle, just your attitude. If you suspect yourself of being your own worst enemy in the war on stress, enroll in yoga or tai-chi, practice meditation, and read some books on positive thinking. At the end of the day it's not worth it! Life really is too short, and worrying about it will only make it shorter!

The Practical Action: *Make a list of all the areas in which you are over or under-stressed, and next to each entry, write down a way in which this may be addressed. Make changes accordingly. Also make a list of things you can do to positively challenge yourself. Some of these things may even be on your first list, but can be re-framed with the benefit of a little relaxation.*

- BL

Angel Rating: 2

75... *clean your granny's curtain rail of dust*

Chances are she can't reach up there and doesn't do well with ladders. I mention the curtain rail cause it's not the most obvious thing, but Granny may be acutely aware of it, and banishing those dust bunnies is important to preserving her dignity. When we care for someone, big sweeping gestures are great, and fantastic for dramatic impact, but it's the little things that can make the difference. If you don't have a granny, find another family member to be nice to!

The Practical Action: *Don't limit yourself to the specificity of this Way. It's surprising how a simple phone call to a relative you haven't spoken to in some time can make a real difference in their day.*

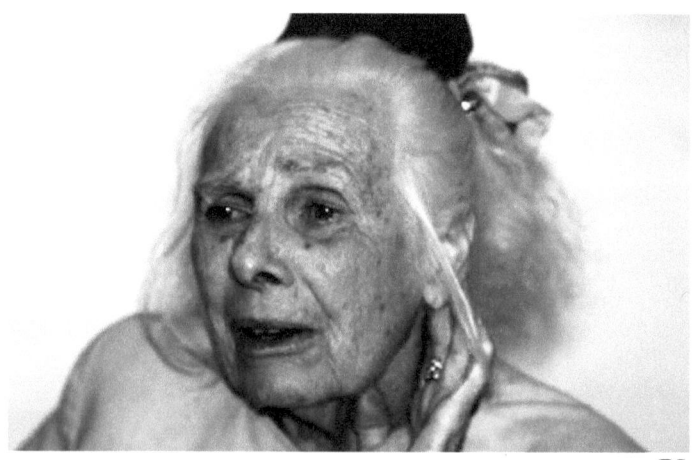

- BL

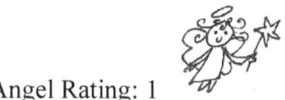

Angel Rating: 1

76...feel free to sing, whistle, and dance (and not only in the shower)

There is a lightness of being that comes with the act of making music. What makes creating a melody particularly attractive is that it can be practiced while doing routine tasks. Walking down the street, sitting in traffic, even doing office work. It has been said that to express music is to open one's own heart beat to others. One of my personal experiences in this category occurred when I was fresh out of college and working at an "upscale" hotel as a fitness attendant. It was a Saturday night, about 8:30, and I was picking up used towels around the pool area and wondering what I was going to do with my life. Then I spotted one of the security guards walking around the pool snapping his fingers. I began to snap mine in unison. He looked up and smiled, and began to do a shuffle dance. I joined him, and he broke into song: *"Sixteen Tons,"* which as an avid listener to old-times classics, I knew the words to as well. We circled the pool, snapping our fingers in matched rhythm and singing about getting *"one day older and deeper in debt."*
When we were done, we were both smiling. Then some applause startled us. Guests had come in from the Marina and stopped to watch us. While there's no miraculously happy ending (such as one of the guests being a record company executive and offering us a recording contract on the spot), this was still definitely one of the most enjoyable moments I had on that job. Though I'm no longer a fitness attendant, I still break into impromptu song and

dance. Do it when things are going great, do it when things are dark. Remember: singing and dancing is a great way to go through life. And extra points if a song you sing is one you wrote yourself. Even if you have no intention of actually recording this tune or having anyone but you hear it. To create words and to then give them voice is a great way of opening yourself up. The song can be a simple refrain, or may tell a story in itself. But there is no such thing as a bad song, providing YOU have written it and YOU sing it. (This does not apply to the majority of pop artists these days polluting the radio airwaves).

The Practical Action: *Start whistling right now, at this moment. Next, think of a song title that describes your past week. It doesn't have to be a cheerful one, but just get it in your mind. Make notes on your week, and see if any lyrics emerge...*

- BP

Angel Rating: 1

If you write out a song and sing it at least once:

77... *elevate consciousness*

We can always go higher. When we do it helps people around us.

One of my shiatsu teachers told us of an ancient Chinese proverb that goes something like this: *"A novice heals by laying on hands, a wise woman can heal with her words, but the sage heals purely by her presence."*

Coming from someone whose job was to teach us massage, it was interesting to know that we were learning the rudest means of healing possible. When we got handed diplomas, at the end of a year and a half of grueling study, they read: *"We hope you aspire to develop your practice further."*

It is the same with the nature of our minds. We might think we're more chill than our neighbors, but let's not get carried away with what we know. Until we reach a point of true revelation and can rest peacefully in a state of calm abiding, we are still just beginning. We must strive to perfect ourselves to the level of the sage, who can elevate the consciousness of any room, just by entering.

The Practical Action: *Meditation, of course. But so you don't get too pretentious thinking about your own elevated consciousness, start with other people. With everyone you meet, start from an assumption that they are a truly realized being – even if their current mode of being does nothing to manifest that. However they are acting, interact as if it's with the realized being that dwells within them. This will help coax that person out!*

- BL

Angel Rating: 2

78... *host a fundraising party*

Parties are fun! Fundraisers are fun and they help raise funds. If your place is no good to host a party, see who you might go to. Get a good team around you if you want to go big. If you want to go glamorous, get a celebrity spokesperson. Pick a worthy cause that people will be happy to write checks to. Fundraisers are a chance to be creative. You can pick any kind of a fun activity and people will enjoy the excuse to go do it. Band gigs are the obvious one, but you could go for square dancing, silly hat bingo, drag-queen Tupperware... the list is endless...

You get to do a good deed and you get to party too.

Incidentally, I approve of parties. I don't think they're too frivolous if done right. If you're living fast, as recommended earlier, I think it's good to throw one every six months so that you can keep up with all the fabulous people you know.

The Practical Action: *Be involved in the organization of at least two parties a year for causes you believe in.*

- BL

Angel Rating: 1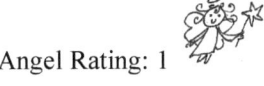

79... *teach a child something*

Sadly, there aren't enough teachers in the world, professional or personal. In a perfect world, school teachers would be making the salaries of professional athletes. However, this not being the case, most teachers I've met teach for the joy of simply seeing their students learn. But you don't have to be teaching for a living in order to experience the pleasure of knowing you've imparted knowledge upon a young person. What to teach them? Well, one should try to avoid skills such as how to hotwire a car or how to build a destructive device. Teach positive, constructive acts: tying one's shoes, swimming, learning how to garden, how to play a musical instrument.... we are blessed with an infinite range of skills we can master. What's important is that you are giving to another a piece of yourself and what you have learned in your time here. Children are indeed precious, and you don't have to be a parent in order to enrich a child's life. Although I'm not a parent, I've got plenty of cousins and I like to think that I've played a role in some aspect of their life. One once told me I inspired her to read. The child of a friend once chuckled at me because I try to use the letter "f" instead of actually curse. However, the next time I saw them they were doing it as well. It was a great feeling. And of course, one is never too old to learn a skill. My Uncle recently instructed me on how to hold a fork properly and "eat like a gentleman" as opposed to my usual method of attacking food.

The Practical Action: *Teach a child something, no matter how trivial it may seem. Also, don't be afraid to allow them to teach you something too, even if you already know how to do it.*

- BP

Angel Rating: 1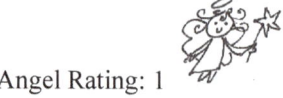

80… *lay your vulnerability on the table*

Talking about awkward subjects brings them out into the open and will help you understand better what's bothering you. With regard to political problems, discussion is an important force for change. Back in England, people wax lyrical on matters of social injustice for hours in the tea room or pub. I don't regard this as a waste of time, more a means to cohere public opinion into a groundswell for change! Of course, they have to pause in drinking tea and beer eventually, and actually do something...

Don't be afraid to share your vulnerabilities, weaknesses and sufferings. To expose yourself without fear to the possibility of ridicule, is to actually show you have strength beyond your faults! By being open about your flaws, you allow people a safe space to talk about theirs, and if they have shame, this will help to lift it. They will feel less alone, and maybe you will too!

The Practical Action: *Confess something you'd never share with a family member to a stranger.*

- BL

BP note: By the way, Blaze, people happen to wax lyrical on social injustices here in America as well. (I should know, being that I've been in more than my share of pubs). As far as

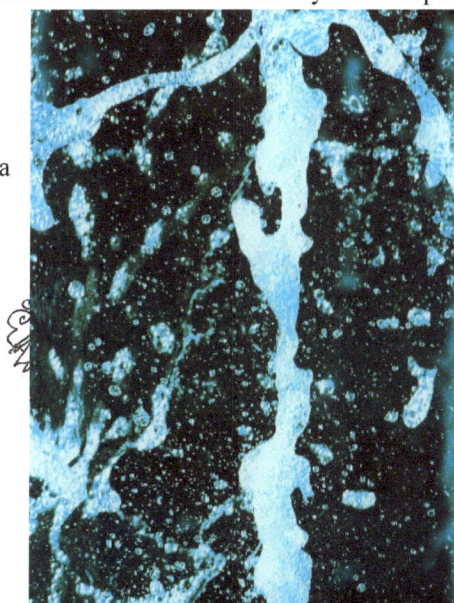

confessing something, let me confess to all that growing up, I was a (gulp) fan of New Kids on the Block.

Angel Rating: 1

81... *vent at*

someone before you actually see them

We all get passionate, and often the closer we are to someone the more intense feelings can be. But sometimes it helps to blow off steam before an actual confrontation. Not only can you practice some cool phrases, you can get any excessive anger out of your system.

So when you do encounter this person, you'll already have a few "takes" of venting under your belt and you'll be able to better concentrate on specific points instead of unleashing a tidal wave. Hemingway was of the opinion that the first draft of a book is like a heated argument with no control whatsoever. Keep in mind that when passion is distilled it becomes that much more coherent and effective. After all, even Shakespeare worked through several drafts of his works. So if you find yourself bubbling over with a temper gone missing, yell and scream to an imaginary person before you encounter the real thing. Not only will you probably make more sense, but you may trim some unnecessary venom from your tirade.

The Practical Action: *Next time you know of an impending confrontation (i.e. a budget meeting, a meeting, a lover's quarrel, etc.), take a few practice runs by yourself and vent your spleen a bit. Act out a scene. Then, when the real one comes, you'll not only be better prepared but a bit less prone to saying something you may regret.*

- BP

Angel Rating: 2

BL note: I'll award you an angel or two if you can avoid even getting to this one. I don't advocate suppressing your anger, however it's very possible, if you're centered and breathe through it, to head your anger off at the pass, and just let it dissipate. Venting rarely helps me, I just get more upset, and I try to exercise caution even with imaginary venting, in case I end up dwelling in a bad mental loop.

BP note: Blaze doesn't know this, but the only way I made it through editing this book with her was to rant and rave before many of our phone calls. By the time we got around to the actual editing, I was as calm as can be.

82... *study quantum physics*

The premise with quantum physics is that everything is interconnected. This is a good way to view the Universe, and can get quite trippy.

For instance, scientists discovered this teeny piece of matter called a wave-particle, that turned out to be mutable according to the intention of the viewer. If the viewer took a look and was expecting to see a wave- form, it would be a wave, if they expected to see a particle, it would be a particle. This is of interest because it raises the idea that our thoughts and intentions have bearing on the Universe at a subatomic level. Expand from here and it can progress to a hypothesis that we create our own destinies, that what we believe, we manifest, that prayers can be answered.

There's been a lot of buzz about this in recent years. I know a bunch of people who were really into that movie, *"The Secret,"* but actually, I found it disappointing that there was so much talk of using intention to manifest wealth and material possessions. My personal feeling is, I can't take quantum physics too seriously where it pertains to the whims of the human ego. We may believe we can fly, but we're still bounden by gravity. And every good runner believes they will win the race, but only one can. I find it more interesting that the Universe might speak to us, than the idea that we might tell the Universe what to do. Yes, I do believe in miracles. But I think it's very rare for any of us to be clear enough that we might truly manifest one. To me, the lesson of quantum physics isn't that we should blaze through the Universe on a Cosmic Schmooze, demanding everything we can from every connection we make, but that we can be gentle in recognition of our interconnectedness, and work to purify our intentions until we give out only love.

Anyway, I'm including it here because it's a good exercise in mind expansion, and you never know, it can't hurt to tap into the flow of the Universe.

The Practical Action: *For further exploration, look at "Synchrodestiny" by Dr Deepak Chopra, the prolific mind-body-spirit author, "The Hidden Messages in Water" by Masuru Emoto. This is a beautiful, even a surprising book, with pictures of water crystals reacting either positively or negatively in response to different words. Also watch the sleeper hit movie "What the Bleep Do We Know?"*

- BL

Angel Rating: 1

83... *politely refuse a telemarketer, and wish them a great night*

Ah, we all know that pause that sometimes greets us after answering the phone. It sounds as if you're talking into a void. Then a person comes on and, amidst the chatter of dozens of other people, mispronounces your name as they ask for you, and then proceeds to offer you a proposal that runs the gamut from a "free trip" to some timeshare resort to a refinance for a loan you don't even have yet. Annoying? Well, yes. But consider this: the person on the other end is most likely in a small cubicle with a headset on, and is doing their job. It's an honest job, one that doesn't pay very well but that does generate revenue for the economy. On a personal note, haven't most of us at one point in our lives found ourselves in jobs that we'd like to consider "beneath us?" I know that when I was working as a telemarketer, I was indeed at a less than stellar point in my life. Chances are if these workers could be doing something else to make a living, they would be. These calls may be a hassle to receive, but think of each as an opportunity to treat with dignity a human being who is struggling, but is still surviving.

The Practical Action: *Treat the next telemarketer who calls you with the same courtesy you'd like to have extended to them if they were a member of your family who happened to have a job as a telemarketer.*

- BP

Angel Rating: 1

BL note: If you're on the "Do Not Call List" as the majority of us are aside from Ben... just try and be nice to everyone who calls, even wrong numbers! If you're not on the list, you can sign up quickly at www.donotcall.gov. It's free!

84... *accept help when you need it, offer help when you don't*

There have been many times traveling in foreign countries when I haven't had a clue where I was going or how I was going to get there. People all over the world have helped me on these occasions, and I have tried to return the favor. Of course this applies to familiar family and friends as well, but if you think about it, as humans we all share a same cognitive link: the ability to give and take help, and the capacity to appreciate the difference both these gestures may make. Accepting help may be hard to do for some; nobody wants to feel powerless. But allowing others to help you can not only serve an immediate need, but also serve as a reminder to you when you are in a position to help others. So don't be too proud to accept help, nor too busy to give it. A friend of mine volunteers at a suicide hotline. She had to undergo a lot of training and it can be, obviously, extremely traumatic at times. But some time ago, while going through what F. Scott Fitzgerald termed "the dark night of the soul," she called a suicide hotline and spoke with someone who was there for her, and thus saved her life. Now, she is there for others.

The Practical Action: *Wait for a time when you can put this into practice. In the meantime, either ask for help programming your DVD player, or ask your ladyfriend to navigate the next time you two take a roadtrip.*

- BP

Angel Rating: 1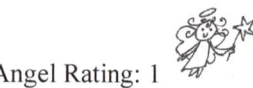

85... *take an eco-vacation*

This is something I always wanted to do but never had the cash – now I have the cash, but I need to wait for my son to grow a bit so he can come too. I hope you read this and take the trip! If you do, I'd love to get a postcard about how great it was!

How to go on an eco-vacation: book through a travel agent that specializes in these things, or start with: www.ecofamilyadventures.com, or www.ecotours.com. There are other sites out there, as this is an expanding market. Different packages offer different opportunities for "voluntourism;" be sure to shop around. Destinations include rainforests in Costa Rica and safari nature preserves in South Africa. Carbon offsets for your flight may be included in the package. (Or you may purchase them separately, see Way #45: "Go Carbon Neutral.")

The cool thing about an eco-vacation are that you get a break from work, get to meet some fantastic like-minded people, and get to do something worthwhile while you're at it. Everyone benefits!

The Practical Action: *Eco-vacation! Can't afford an eco-vacation? See if you can make it out to New Orleans for a few days to help rebuild. www.habitat-nola.org, or www.pnola.org,*

- BL

Angel Rating: 1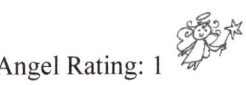

86... *attune yourself to the elevation of planetary consciousness*

If you believe, as I do, that our job whilst on this Earth is to perfect ourselves spiritually, then this opens you to the possibility that the human consciousness is evolving to a higher level. It would be easy to believe the opposite; the planet is in peril, we're still at war, the power is wielded by faceless mega-corporations, terrible things are happening... In spite of all these things, if you look, people everywhere are still doing incredibly cool things, and pretty much, we just want to be happy and fulfilled. Once you accept the idea that there can be a quickening in the human consciousness, you will see evidence of the endless potentiality out there.

This is a dark time within the history of the world. It is literally up to the weight of individuals to define consumer interests, to decide whether the climate crisis will reach tipping point, or if the Earth will be brought back from the brink of disaster. As in a siege situation, when people rally together for the common good, I believe this can bring people together in unprecedented acts of goodwill. Cynics would see it as we need to join forces for purposes of self-preservation, but actually there's immense opportunity at this time, for people to really change the way we think and interact and behave.

Under the Gaia hypothesis, the biosphere is a network of complex eco-systems that must remain in balance in order to sustain life. The global village gives us more opportunity to witness this than ever before. And whilst human actions are impacting negatively on the biosphere, our human spirits can work positively to raise the global consciousness.

Believe that the planetary consciousness is rising, and attune yourself to that elevation.

You are riding the wave of the upsurge!

101 Ways to Get Into Heaven

The Practical Action: *Form a group of positive thinkers to meditate on this very idea. Give it some concentrated thought. You can do bi-monthly or monthly sessions, or weekly if there's a catastrophe going on.*

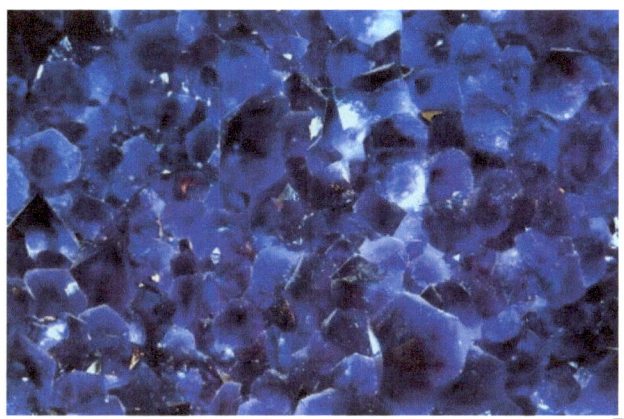

- BL

Angel Rating: 2

87... *eat good food, and don't forget to nourish your soul*

Of course it's good to be health conscious. We've a duty to look after our bodies if they're to perform to their optimum levels. You should get an Angel Token for this part, no problem, it's basic self-care and very simple.

A lot of things are very simple; according to Monty Python, the Meaning of Life is to, *"Uh, try and be nice to people, avoid eating fat, read a good book every now and then, get some walking in, and try and live together in peace and harmony with people of all creeds and nations."*

I had to throw that in there because it's so simple it's trite, which makes it funny, but still, humanity hasn't quite managed the latter part.

I feel like I should give some healthy eating tips here, but really, I've only one: Cut down on dead animals! If you're not ready to go vegetarian, at least reduce your consumption. Vegan kids are taller and smarter than omnivores, vegan adults are healthier and live about a decade longer. And as far as the "thou shalt not kill" thing, not eating meat spares about 83 animals a year. Not to mention you're curbing harmful emissions and slowing climate change. Good for all concerned, and for body, mind and spirit! For a free starter kit with recipes and tips, go to www.goveg.com.

Anyway, back to my point about spiritual health consciousness, our souls need nourishing in the same way as our bodies. And being as a body won't work without a soul in it, it stands to reason that if a soul gets sick, the body will get sick too. When you feel life is dragging you down despite your best efforts, do something to lift yourself up. This may be a visit to the park, gallery, theater, - or a trip to volunteer at the local hospice. Just do something. It's not indulgent. Looking at cute furry animals on the internet only takes a minute. Go to You can sneak a look while you're meant to be working! If you're a tough type like me, though, don't mention it to your significant other.

- BL

Angel Rating - for eating a meatless meal: 1

Angel Rating - for going vegan: 3 FAT ANGELS!

88... *whatever your gifts may be, think of ways to give back*

This sounds like a generalization for a reason: you are a gift to the world that is uniquely you. No one can tell you what your specialness is, only you can find it and work it to the max. Follow your bliss. Therein lies a talent that will liberate you and can help save the world! (A hint here. Aim high. Lower chakra stuff may help you win a hot dog eating contest, but it doesn't really give back. Unless you hurl, and who wants to see that...?)

By contributing your unique talents, you create a rich and diverse world for us all to enjoy. So celebrate!

- Hopefully you won't you draw a blank on this one, but if you do, throw a birthday party so all your friends can celebrate you! This won't save the world, but it will probably boost your self-esteem.

The Practical Action: *It's hard to be specific here, as I don't know what your talents are. A small example would be, I know how to make twisty balloons, and can volunteer to make wiener dogs any time there's a gathering of children! Also, I've good hair, so when I grow a long pony tail, I can cut it off and send it to make wigs for chemotherapy patients.*

- BL

Angel Rating: 1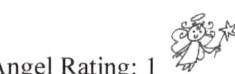

89... *let go*

Here's a quote from T.S. Eliot: *"I said to my soul, be still, and wait without hope. For hope would be hope for the wrong thing; and wait without love, for love would be love of the wrong thing; there is yet faith."*

Too much attachment to anything can be a bad thing. All of your hopes, fears, and expectations can make you suffer. It is for this reason that I urge you to put yourself out there in a gesture of good faith, and to believe that the gesture is everything, not the outcome.

I can't proselytize about this one; this is actually very hard to achieve. It's very human to want, and most of us aren't saintly enough to get past this in a hurry. But I think this is one of the most relevant things in here, because desire is the root of so much of our pain!

Be aware, that when you're on your ascent to Heaven, that nothing that you attach to will be of relevance. The outcome of all of the actions you accumulated on Earth will be of no relevance. All that will matter will be the purity of the intentions behind them.

Actually, this is very comforting. If you have truly made an effort at life, chances are you have experienced a lot of failure. These failures sting at the time, but your ability to absorb them is a measure of the love you hold inside you. Only the love matters. The love makes you Divinely successful!

It's important to note, with regard to letting go, that it's okay to want all kinds of things, so long as you do so selflessly. So keep wanting, just not too much. Persevere. It will be worth it.

The Practical Action: *Whatever dreams, expectations and things you are most attached to, imagine how your life would be without them. Chances are, it wouldn't be a disaster, and you'd still be a pretty good person! (If that latter doesn't hold true, re-prioritize your life!)*

- BL

Angel Rating: 2

90… *passionately declare your love for someone*

As was stated in the musical *Les Miserables,* *"To love another person is to see the face of God."* Indeed. Should you find yourself captured by this miracle, don't be afraid

to shout it from the rooftops! Be it through poetry, speech, growing a plant for them, or

giving them a living creature to care for. Unexpected flowers. Whisper it in their ear while they sleep. Most everyone in this world has known hurt, and it's courageous to open your heart to another. To declare love for another is also to declare love for yourself, as someone worthy of committing to this insanely confusing, but completely worthwhile emotion.

The Practical Action: *Today, tell another living being that you love them.*

- BP

Angel Rating: 1

91... create sacred space for your home and family

I'm not talking about setting up an altar or a place for retreat, although both of these are fantastic things to do and will help. The space I'm talking about is inward. We all have thoughts, and a lot of them. Learn to be spacious with your thoughts. That gap between thoughts is the sacred space I'm referring to. It's sacred in the same way that "silence is golden" - because it allows us to cultivate a clarity of thought. Instead of your thoughts tumbling onward in a confused stampede, they can stop and form an orderly line. The ones that weren't important will likely dismiss themselves. Clearing your headspace will also allow you to relax your ego. In the gap between thoughts, you won't be thinking about all the niggling things your mind was grasping on to, and this may allow you space for more important stuff, like considering others, being of service, and seeing what's really going on.

Be spacious. If you're no good with this, seek out a meditation class. The group energy will carry you.

The Practical Action*: This can work for your whole family! If you really want to get into it together, go to:* www.kerryleemaclean.com*. This is a family-friendly website where you can "Meditate with the Piggies." It's funny and cute. Kerry Lee Maclean is author of "The Family Meditation Book," and other kid-related fare.*

- BL

Angel Rating: 1

92... *shop wisely*

I've been procrastinating on writing on this one, as it's so encompassing.

Yeah, be careful what you wish for, or you might get it and find it was made by child slaves. I know, the very notion is horrific. Unfortunately it happened to me. It turns out that the majority of the world's cocoa beans are picked by stolen children, who are sold for about a buck-fifty and subjected to wretched conditions. Just google *"chocolate"*, *"child slavery"* plus the current year, and you'll see. Did I mention I'm a chocoholic? I felt betrayed when I found out! Luckily I can still get my fix by buying "fair-trade" and organic chocolate.

In a consumer society, the labor problem permeates so many aspects of our lives. Even in Los Angeles, illegal sweatshops are knocking out designer rip-offs. This is shocking because it's local, but sweatshops are prevalent in developing nations. Virtually anything made in China, which is most of the stuff for sale in the rest of the world, may have been manufactured under sweatshop conditions. The sad thing is, the goods are selling because of the bargain prices made possible by the low manufacturing costs.

Another thing to consider when you purchase is the environmental impact of your goods; cars, paint, detergent, tables, burgers all fall into this category. Green alternatives are explained at www.greenerchoices.org, Green businesses are listed at www.coopamerica.org.

Also, animals get exploited as well as people! For a list of "cruelty free" companies, go to: www.caringconsumer.com/resources_companies.asp.

It's up to you to weigh up the cheapness of the item against the human and animal and environmental costs. I sympathize if this is difficult for you. I try to boycott where I can, but it's a hard thing to explain when your child wants a toy.

Do what you can.

The Practical Action: *By being informed and empowered consumers, we can help dictate to market forces: Use your monetary power to buy into a better future.*

- BL

Angel Rating: 3

93… *find your point of epiphany*

I can't actually tell you where this is, so here's a quick poem of mine:

101 Ways to Get Into Heaven

Be as a mirror at the point where –

The sun rises and a flower opens,

Clouds burst and water wells,

Where sap drips sticky as

The red fruit ripens red;

The valleys plunge and mountains reach,

A woman and a man reach to one another,

A gift is given and received.

At this intersection point,

The Universe meets and blesses itself.

Cherish this place and put your heart there,

To shine many turning reflections!

I know this is a bit ethereal. I hope that wasn't too pretentious. Maybe what I meant was something like this: Always be embracing. Always feel embraced. Always be learning. Always be growing. Don't be afraid of getting it wrong. If you do, know that your biggest opportunities for growth are in moments of shock or embarrassment.

Albert Camus had this to say about the matter: *"Live to the point of tears."*

The Practical Action: *Next time you find yourself in an "epiphany moment," just breathe, and allow yourself to experience it fully. Remember that moment and go back to that feeling in your daily actions. Encourage more like it!*

Angel Rating: 1

94... *feed a hungry person*

There's no shame in being hungry. Food is indeed a basic need. True, some who beg are mentally unstable, and many do have substance abuse problems. But there are also a fair amount of those who have simply fallen on hard times. A loaf of bread, a taco, a candy bar... any kind of sustenance feeds not only the body but, if given by another, the spirits of not only the recipient but also the provider.

The Practical Action: *The next time anyone asks you for money, offer to buy them some food.*

- BP

Angel Rating: 1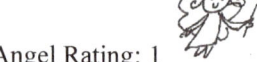

95... *share your thoughts in order that others may share theirs*

Talk is cheap, but don't you be. Be conversationally generous. I'm not talking about gossiping, I'm talking about sharing the crème-de-la-crème-de-your-consciousness. Share the good thoughts, compliments, and fond contemplations. It will lift people up. Sometimes people are afraid to speak out, for fear of appearing too emotional/ambitious/political/intellectual. I say we need more of all these things! Speak out and it will encourage others. If you have deep philosophical musings in your breast, let them out! (Or get a bigger bra.)

Be aware that conversational generosity is a two-way street. Don't let your thoughts pour forth uninterrupted, or open your mouth without first engaging your brain. Allow yourself to pause. It is good for your mental health to leave space between thoughts. In conversation, your pause is a space in which to listen to the other person. They have important things to say.

The Practical Action: *Next time you are in a group and one member seems particularly reticent, see if you can draw them out by giving your opinion on something. It may be as simple as how nice their shoes are! Follow up by asking them a question.*

- BL

Angel Rating: 1

96... go on a complaint-free diet

Complaining can be addictive. It can become all too easy to blame outside forces for one's current situation than taking a good look around and within. If we make a conscious decision to not complain, we can see situations in a whole new light. You can reach a point at which you cease to attach to all the things you were griping about and realize that either they weren't so important, or that they're worth fighting for and you can come up with a plan of action to achieve real change. Either way, you may discover there are more constructive ways to spend your time than complaining

The Practical Action: *Try to go a week without complaining. If you catch yourself in the middle of a complaint, cease and say the words "God Bless It." Hopefully these words will remind you that, down the road, you'll look back and remember fondly that you had the luxury of so many things to complain about.*

- BL

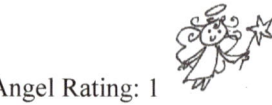

Angel Rating: 1

97... *try to understand something you really hate about someone*

You really can't change other people. That's up to them. If you don't want to get frustrated about the situation, it's best to try and understand it. Generally when it gets to the level where I hate something about someone, it defies comprehension, actually, but it's still good to try and break it down. Consider that we all share a common thread of humanity: Just as everyone is capable of suffering, everyone at some level is trying to find a way to be happy, no matter how misguided their efforts.

It's also good to separate out the hatefulness from the person. A case in point: I think George Bush is a war criminal and have disliked every most all of his decisions. But even he has made the effort, on three occasions, to meet with His Holiness the Dalai Lama, a man who's the epitome of peace and compassion. So George isn't all bad. I'm not saying that all he needs is a good cuddle and he'll get better, it's more complicated than that. But somewhere inside, there's a frightened human being who is worthy of love, ha-ha!

The Practical Action: *The next time you are disgusted with the actions of another, ask yourself if there is something fueling that person you may not understand. If possible, ask them why they behave as they do. If not possible, just know that they are a human being who is trying, maybe too desperately, to find happiness.*

- BL

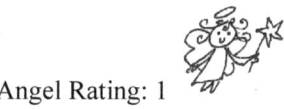

Angel Rating: 1

98... *write your leaders*

Show you have a voice and write your Representatives on the issues you care about. You will get a letter back, I guarantee it!

The Internet makes it very easy to write people, and it's free to do so long as you have access to a computer.

Check out: www.thepetitionsite.com, and www.change.org

There's online petitions and you can sign up with a lot of worthy causes to get "action alerts." These are periodic emails to tell you of email campaigns on issues you care about. When you sign up you just fill out a form just once, and the next time you click, it will autofill and jet your letter instantaneously to its recipient. If you're into doing a bunch of these, have an email account dedicated for that purpose. Friends will email you with more of them, it could all mount up. If it all mounts up, set a specific time each week, where you can breeze through it quickly. I aim for Sundays after my kid goes to bed. Somehow my kid got hip to it too, and even though he can't quite write yet, he can't wait to write the President!

- BL

The Practical Action: *Go on, write the President!*

Angel Rating: 1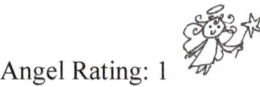

99... ask God to help with the vacuuming

I've been in the habit, when I pray, of praying mostly for the big things, like world peace, an end to hunger and enlightenment for everyone. Such things aren't prayers that get answered quickly, but I figure by praying I'm doing my bit. Then I'll get into generalizations like good health and happiness for my family and friends. Which are smaller in scale and more easily fulfilled. Mostly I try not to request anything selfish, it seems ignoble.

Anyway, I was trying to do some Spring cleaning the other day, and just about got lost down a rabbit hole of dust bunnies. The place was in such a state of disarray I was ready to despair. Normally I wouldn't pray for anything so trivial and selfish as the strength to clean my house, but then it occurred to me, why shouldn't I, if it was really getting me down? Immediately I felt relief. Of course the Divine could help me get my house in order – this was a very small request and one that I was willing to personally put in the work on. Sometimes the best prayers are the ones that fall under our own jurisdiction.

So how, may you ask, if I was the one wielding the vacuum cleaner, did praying about it change anything? The difference was in my perspective. Instead of being victim to my own stress and rebellion, I could recognize the Divine order at work even in my household! This is a powerful thing! Imagine, if it is God's will that dust bunnies be banished from your house, who are you to argue?

The Practical Action: *Recognize that there is no such thing as a trivial prayer, just as there is no such thing as a trivial action, or a trivial life.*

- BL

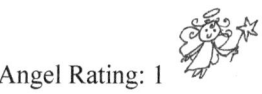

Angel Rating: 1

100... *accept that you are one day going to pass on from this life*

There's an ancient ninja saying that reads, *"You have been granted a death so that you may realize the startling significance of why you are here as a human being, and not as a cooking pot."* Ladies and gentlemen, you are a human being. It stands to reason the karma we build up in this life will follow us to whatever may lie next. YOU can make a difference in people's lives. You don't have to write a brilliant novel, discover a cure for a dreaded disease, or rescue a person from a burning building. Faith need not be absolute: even Mother Teresa had doubts about her own faith, and battled with the accursed blessing of being human. We all have doubts, we all have nightmares, we all have demons. But it is our choice to, before we leave this current incarnation, either enhance people's lives or cripple them.

Presumably you're reading this book because you are a practical person, unsure of any ironclad text or religion that will earn you a ticket to Heaven.

Well, bad news and good news. We don't know any concrete way to get into Heaven, either. Not only that, but we are all going to die one day.

The Good news is that as you read this you are alive. Today, at this moment, capable of taking another step toward Heaven.

       Act accordingly.   - BP

The Practical Action*: Don't get all gothy,or anything, but just think about it.*

Angel Rating: 1

101... *experience Heaven in the moment*

Congratulations! You made it through this book! No doubt you're well on your way to Heaven now!! You made it all the way up the Spirit Level chart? That's great! We know pride is a sin, but we want to say how proud we are of you!

One last word: Don't get complacent about your level of realization. Once attained, it must be maintained. It's all very well to commune with nature, but if you curse out your neighbor's dog the day after, you need to go back to the well. And there are many levels of realization. I'm sure you're happy to know you're going to Heaven now. When you get your bearings, see how many people you can take with you. Keep doing what you've been doing. You've done great!

There is a level of Heaven, beyond the Seventh, that's off the chart!! You don't even need to die to get there, though your ego might! Heaven is right here around us, now and forever. We can't go looking for it, it's bumping us on the nose! If we can only develop the clarity to see it, it is there for us and always was. Like William Blake said, *"If the doors of perception were cleansed, everything would appear to man as it is, infinite."*

Breathe deep. Exalt quietly. You can experience Heaven in the moment. And the moment reaches beyond time and space, to embrace infinity.

- BL

The Practical Action: *Come up with your own practical action! It's all on you!*

Angel Rating: 1-FAT

ABOUT THE AUTHORS

BLAZE LOVEJOY has unabashed dreams of world peace and planetary healing. She believes the power to elevate the human consciousness is within us all.

Originally from England, Blaze has worked variously as a journalist, health columnist and poet. Years of working as a shiatsu therapist have given her a strong background in New Age disciplines and the healing arts. She has also worked as a Campaign Coordinator in the non-profit sector, with "Friends of the Earth," "Greenpeace," and "Pensioners Link." She tries to keep busy with worthy causes and is conversant on issues of environment, world hunger and human and animal rights. She is Co-President of the company, "Hungry Yak Productions," through which she has written and produced the films "God's Waiting List," and "Actual Images: The Valley Murders." (The latter is a satire against media violence.) She has taught classes in creative writing, massage certification and "Spiritual Filmmaking." She is a Minister of "The Universal Life Church."

Blaze lives in Los Angeles, with her family and four cats. She drives for free, in a three-wheeled, zebra-striped car that plugs into her solar-powered house. If you see her on the road, chances are, you will smile!

BEN PELLER, after experiencing a life-threatening health crisis, has frantically reconsidered the ungodly amount of mistakes he's made in life, and has since learned that living well is not only the best revenge, but a good way to help others and also prepare for what may come once our time in this dimension is finished. He is the author of the novel "Living the Gimmick," and has read poetry across the country from Big Sur to New Orleans. He stays fit and lively through a stringent routine of exercise and nutritional supplements and a strict abstinence from reality television.

Ben gives blood every 58 days, and has managed to reside in Los Angeles for the past decade without owning either a car or a cellphone. If you see him on the road, please don't cut him off, as cyclists are vulnerable.

SPIRIT LEVEL CHART

Level	Description	Reward
Heavenly Realm	You are ready to ascend!	Throw a party!!
Gold Aura Level	You are vibrant with inner radiance!	Kiss Somebody!
Silver Cord Level		Get a Massage
Crown Chakra Level	You embrace higher potentialities!	Buy a CD or download of your choice
Third-eye Chakra Level	You awaken to new awareness!	Take a bubble bath!
Throat Chakra Level	You express yourself freely and creatively!	Get paint or a new Pen!
Heart Chakra Level	You are open to give and receive love.	Go out on a Nice date!
Spleen Chakra Level	You reach new understandings.	Light a scented candle.
Navel Chakra Level	You are becoming more centered.	Eat fair trade Chocolate!
Root Chakra Level	Congratulations! You are embarking on your journey!	Buy new Shoes!

Conscience meter: ☐☐☐☐☐☐☐☐☐☐

101 Ways to Get Into Heaven

How to Use the Spirit Level Chart is explained in the front of the book.

Have a glorious time!

Here are the tokens for the chart (or draw your own however you'd like!):

Angel token:

Fat Angel:

Guilty conscience sticker: ☹

Absolution sticker: ☺

Grace token:

Here's a ray of light on a chilly day, to say:

Thank you for all your good karmas!

All our love,

Ben and Blaze

www.ingramcontent.com/pod-product-compliance
Lightning Source LLC
Chambersburg PA
CBHW041621220426
43662CB00001B/11